W9-BNH-335

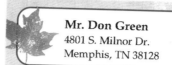

Mr. Don Green
4801 S. Milnor Dr.
Memphis, TN 38128

FRONTIER
SKILLS

FRONTIER
SKILLS
The Tactics and Weapons that
Won the American West

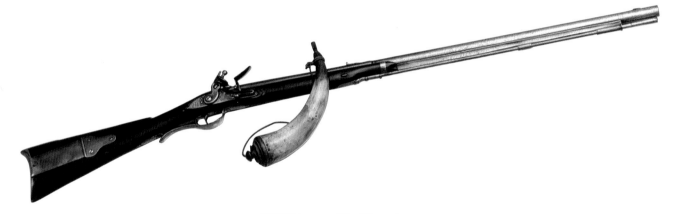

William C. Davis

THE LYONS PRESS

A Salamander Book

Published in the United States by The Lyons Press
Guilford, CT 06437
www.lyonspress.com
An imprint of The Globe Pequot Press

© Salamander Books Ltd., 2003

A member of **Chrysalis** Books plc

ISBN 1 58574 679 7

1 3 5 7 9 8 6 4 2

All rights reserved. Except for use in a review, no part of this book may be reproduced, stored in
a retrieval system or transmitted in any form or by any means, electronic, mechanical,
photocopying or otherwise, without prior permission of Salamander Books Ltd.

All correspondence concerning the content of this volume should be addressed to Salamander Books Ltd.

The Author

William C. Davis is the author or editor of more than forty books in the fields of American (in particular Southern)
history and the Civil War, as well as numerous documentary screenplays. He has twice been nominated for the
Pulitzer Prize in History, and is the only three-time winner of the Jefferson Davis Award given for book-length works
on Confederate history. Among his many acclaimed works are *The West*, *The American Frontier*, and the
Rebels & Yankees Civil War trilogy, all for Salamander. His many broadcasting assignments have included acting
as on-camera senior consultant for fifty-two episodes of the Arts & Entertainment Network/History Channel series
"Civil War Journal." Davis is Director of Programs for the new Virginia Center for Civil War Studies
at Virginia Tech, as well as serving as Professor of History.

Credits

Project Manager: Ray Bonds
Designer: Heather Moore
Artifact photography: Don Eiler
Reproduction: Anorax Imaging Ltd.
Printed in China

Acknowledgments

The publishers are grateful to the many private collectors and various institutions that have provided artifacts
and/or illustrations shown in this book. They include American Heritage Center, University of Wyoming, Laramie;
American Museum of Natural History; Anchorage Museum of History and Art, Anchorage; Arizona Historical Society,
Tucson; Buffalo Bill Historical Center, Cody, Wyoming; Colonial National Historical Park, Yorktown, Va.;
Colorado Historical Society, Denver; The Church of Jesus Christ of Latter-Day Saints, Salt Lake City;
California Section, California State Library, Sacramento; Denver Public Library, Western History Department, Denver;
Kansas State Historical Society, Topeka; Metropolitan Museum of Art, New York; Minnesota Historical Society;
Montana Historical Society, Helena; National Archives; Nebraska State Historical Society;
Smithsonian Institution, Washington, D.C.; University of Pennsylvania Museum, Philadelphia.

Additional captions: Page 2, many professional trappers turned their attention and their guns onto the buffalo on the
plains when the demand for beaver hats declined in the East. Page 3, Harpers Ferry Model 1803 flintlock rifle, .54 caliber,
with horn, the type of longarm that would have been carried by some members of the Lewis and Clark expedition.

Contents

Introduction ~ 6

Indian Survival Skills ~ 12

The First European Arrivals ~ 24

The Explorers ~ 32

The Mountain Men ~ 44

Overland Emigrant Trains ~ 56

Hunters and Settlers ~ 72

The Frontier Army ~ 88

Men at War ~ 100

The End of the Frontier ~ 114

Endnotes ~ 126

Index ~ 127

Introduction

IN SEPTEMBER 1827 the notorious land speculator James Bowie of Louisiana took part in one of the most famous of all Mississippi River brawls, the so-called "Sandbar Fight," actually fought on a sand bar in the river near Natchez. He emerged with his life, but just barely. He was shot twice, once through the lung, stabbed in fourteen places with sword canes, one thrust puncturing one of his lungs, and given a nasty hash on the head by a thrown pistol. Many thought he would not survive the night. "Butchered as I was," he said six years later, "it was long before I recovered from the injuries." Eventually the wounds healed enough to allow him to continue his adventurous life, but as late as 1831, by which time he had moved to Texas, his head still ached from the pistol wound, and refused to heal completely.

He met an old hunter who told him to kill a bear, then cut out its stomach, and make it into a cap with a hole in the top. He should wear the "maw," as he called it, and pour bear fat oil into the hole every morning. In time the head would heal. Not finding a bear immediately, Bowie tried it with a deer's stomach, which only dried out and stiffened, hurting his scalp even more. But then one day he found a fat bear, killed it, made the hat, and began pouring in the oil. "In a short time, my head was well, and troubled me no more," he told a friend, thus preserving his head for a little more than another four years before Mexican bullets blew his brains out at the Alamo.*

However spectacularly unsuccessful Bowie was at surviving when confronted by Mexican muskets, his use of the bear's maw cap – whether it actually had anything to do with healing his head or not – is just one example of the ways, sometimes seemingly bizarre, that the people of the frontier tried to cope with the hazards of their lifestyles and environments. Folk medicines and cures could be just as important as skill with weapons or woodcraft in preserving life. Virtually all who lived in the vast expanse west of the Mississippi during the century between 1800 and 1900 encountered a host of challenges to their longevity and successful tenure in this new West.

Above: *Prospectors in camp at Cunningham Gulch, San Juan County, Colorado. Many came west seeking new lives and fortunes. Only the resilient succeeded, especially those who chose to brave such a rugged and unforgiving wilderness.*

*"A Fortnight with James Bowie by the Rev. Benjamin Chase," Alamo Journal (William C. Davis, ed.), #126 (September 2002), p. 4.

Above: *Those who survived in the hard land often had to improvise to meet the most extreme conditions, like this Koryak girl who has chiseled through lake ice and is fishing through the hole. In such an environment, they competed not just with other humans but animals for food.*

Indeed, no other period in its past presented nearly so many obstacles and dangers, simply because never before did no many people of different cultures, with differing habits and ambitions, compete – often with each other – to make a place for themselves there.

The native peoples had been there for millennia, of course, and were accustomed through ancient experience and habit to what they needed to know and do to survive. Moreover, they were good at it. They had found a natural equilibrium between themselves and their neighbors, and the environment itself, to establish and preserve a coexistence that, if not always peaceful, still favored the long-term survival of the great body of their peoples. Their greatest enemy was not one another, but climate, which could dramatically affect everything from their drinking water to the migration of the bison herds upon which many depended.

By contrast, when the white Europeans began filtering onto the map west of the Mississippi, they brought other ancient ways and expectations that were almost totally at odds with the wilderness and its peoples. Two thousand years earlier their ancestors had faced similar challenges in the Old World, but the ensuing centuries of

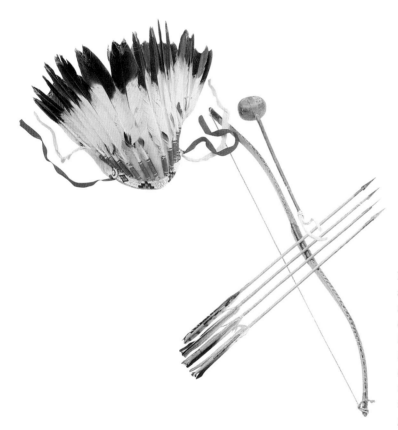

Left: *For the Northern Cheyenne man, his tools of survival were also those for war, and were emblems of his tribal culture as well. Here a bald eagle feather headdress, a bow covered in bull snake skin, eagle-fletched arrows with steel tips, and a stone-headed war club, make up the essential weaponry for hunt or battle.*

Western civilization had removed almost all such forces from their daily lives. Thus, when they came to the West, they would have to learn again what they had forgotten, as well as a host of new skills specially fitted for this often unforgiving landscape and its frequently harsh weather.

Moreover, in the inevitable contest with the native inhabitants of this territory, the Europeans would have to learn new ways of warfare as well. They were accustomed to facing each other by a set of rules almost universal in the Old World. But the Indians had established their own rules geared to staying alive here. Thus, when the two combatants met in hostilities, whether an isolated skirmish by a handful of men, or in pitched battles, the fact that neither played by the same code of ethics or rituals meant that each would have to learn the ways of the other in order to survive.

Indeed, it was this mixture of accommodation of the reality presented by the West, with the skills inherent to the several cultures that challenged this country, which determined not who would survive necessarily, but rather how those who did survive addressed the problem. Even raw numbers were not enough in the early years, for exposure to an unknown microbe could level the playing field with dramatic swiftness, just as could a flood, an avalanche, or a wild forest fire.

Survival, moreover, was just as much a collective matter as one for the individual. Whole tribes of Indians would disappear forever because they faced challenges and circumstances they could no longer overcome, regardless of who was responsible. The frontiersman who did admirably on his own out in the wild – and they were many fewer of these consummate individualists than Western lore would have it – still had to know how to co-operate as part of a joint effort in a fort or village, where all the rules of survival changed dramatically. Even once the plains were tamed by the fence and the plow, and the mountains girdled by rails and roads, still that spirit of community and common cause remained essential for the bettered outlook for prosperity and longevity of the mass.

In the end, regardless of age, gender, race or nationality, survival on this frontier would come down to basic attributes that had always

been essential through the whole history of human experience – endurance, strength, ingenuity, co-operation, and simple unwillingness to give up. Everyone who came to the West had all these and more. Those who did not did not stay or survive long. Even many of those who came but failed still had them, but simply found themselves pitted against others with greater advantages. Years before the followers of Charles Darwin coined the phrase, the American West was acting as a proving ground for the adage "survival of the fittest." There was nothing either fair or equitable about it. Only the land itself was impartial. Beyond that, they were all on their own.

William C. Davis, 2003

Above: *The way west looked romantic to many a pilgrim before the journey, and has been heavily romanticized since, as in Emanuel Leutze's 1862 painting "Westward the Course of Empire Takes its Way." Virtually every sort of westering character is depicted, yet this is the West of the imagination, not the West of men and women struggling and scrapping just to survive against man and the elements.*

CHAPTER ONE

Indian Survival Skills

"Anyone living in the region needed warm clothes and shelter,
strategies for food storage, a means of traveling over snow and ice."
(Natalie Tobert, Hornimans Museum London, on the Americas during the Ice Age)

Below: *For the Plains Indians – as indeed for many other native peoples – survival meant the bison, and when they were all but gone, the tribes that looked to them for food, clothing, shelter, and more had nowhere else to turn. The fading of the buffalo here symbolizes the waning of the Indian way of life.*

STEREOTYPES, FOR ALL their overdrawn excess, often contain the germ of truth at their root. Humorist Mark Twain once satirized the novels of James Fennimore Cooper for their portrayal of Indians. When an Iroquois stepped on a twig, it never snapped. When he walked on a path, he left no print. When he strung an arrow to his bow or threw his tomahawk, he never missed, and his eyes, ears, and nose were always seemingly reading things in his environment that no white man could detect. Cooper's natives are romanticized idealizations of the aboriginal inhabitants of early America, his

caricatures heavily influenced by the ethos of the "noble savage" then in vogue in American and European culture. Yet Twain perhaps protested too much all the same, for there were large grains of truth in the survival skills demonstrated by the Deerslayer's Indian friends and enemies.

The skills developed by the first Americans for surviving in a vast and largely unfriendly environment are known to us only by inference and deduction prior to their initial encounters with Europeans who recorded native practices. However, there is little reason to suspect that such skills would have been any different before the coming of the white man, for they were the same basic attributes common to virtually all Stone Age peoples around the globe. At their root they were little different from the skills and instincts practiced even by most mammals, both carnivorous hunters and herbivorous prey alike. Yet to the earliest white visitors to North America – people whose culture had long before evolved away from basic survival skills – the methods of the Indians seemed strange, even inhuman.

Above: An early woodcut depicts a battle between the Iroquois and a body of Huron, Montagnais, and Ottawa, assisted by Frenchmen under Samuel de Champlain with their muskets in 1609. The arrival of white men with guns completely changed the survival equation for native peoples.

For all of the contexts in which whites would have occasion to observe native behavior, most of their survival skills seemed to be encapsulated in their way of making war – an activity in which European and aboriginal peoples in early America would unhappily spend so much of their time together for four centuries. The French explorer Antoine de la Mothe Cadillac captured much of it in his perplexed, condescending, and yet rather admiring description of an Ottawa attack on a rival tribe in the early 1700s. "One might say that these people are guided by instinct rather than by knowledge or reason," he thought. When the Ottawa moved into their foe's territory, they moved without the fanfare of a European army. "They go warily," he found. "They keep silence, observe everything, and never shoot firearms." He marveled that, when they crossed the trail of another unseen party, they could tell if the trail was fresh or old, could guess the number of men who had passed and how long before, and, knowing their own speed on foot, they could estimate where that enemy now would be. He swore that they could even tell from a footprint the tribe of the man who made it.

Truly it seemed that the Ottawa – and by extension virtually all woodland peoples – could move without noise and read the invisible. When they were on the trail of a foe, "if a man or a number of men are discovered," felt Cadillac, "their doom is almost certain and unfailing." No one who was not skilled in Indian ways could escape them. "You may walk on moss or leaves, or through marshes, or even over rocks, but all precautions you take to conceal your track are quite useless, for the pursuers are rarely at fault." Their foe finally in sight, even then the Ottawa did not signal their arrival, nor form line of battle, beat drums, and march to engage as Europeans expected. Instead, they quietly studied the foe's camp by night, then debated among themselves the best means of attacking with maximum damage to the foe and minimal risk to themselves. Once they decided their chances were good, then they suited action to word and sped away at once in the darkness. Then, when within sight of their quarry, they simply lay down on the ground, protecting their position with outposts of their own to guard against surprise, and waited for sunrise, believing that sleeping men had the greatest difficulty in

Below: *The native peoples became remarkably adept at adapting materials at hand to the work of eking their survival out of the wilderness. The Aleuts of present-day Alaska made spears like this one for taking the seabirds that flocked along the coast. They made spear points of sharpened bone and embedded them in wooden shafts.*

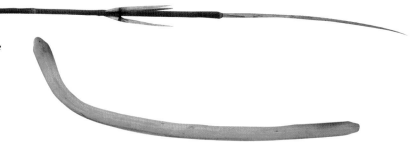

Right: *Among the more imaginative weapons for taking game were these throwing sticks used by the Diegueño Indians for killing rabbits. The skill necessary to use them effectively is a tribute to perseverance, and necessity.*

14

rousing themselves just before dawn.

"Their custom is to drag themselves along on the ground on all fours like cats and approach within pistol shot," Cadillac continued. Then they stood erect, and when their leader gave a signal – still not loud enough to stir the camp – they let out a chilling war shout and fired their arrows, or muskets if they had them. If that volley and their whoops confused or panicked the men in the camp, then the Ottawa rushed in with knives and tomahawks, made quick work of as many as they could, took scalps as war trophies when possible, and brought out prisoners before the rest of their quarry could regroup. Then they immediately set out at a fast pace to retrace their steps to the safety of their own villages. It was almost a template for every Indian raid made from Atlantic to Pacific, from Mexico to Canada, and across time from unrecorded antiquity to the end of the Indian wars late in the 1800s.[1]

Native people applied precisely the same skills to the hunting that provided them with meat, using careful reconnaissance, patience and stealth, knowledge of the ground, and surprise to achieve their ends whether in a hunting group in the dense deer forests of the East, or a mounted party after bison on the plains. And when aware that an enemy was on their trail, those very same attributes helped them to prevent surprise, to counter an attack with one of their own, or to endeavor to make their own passage through the wilderness as undetectable as possible. Most of all, what enabled them to develop such skills was awareness born of lifelong intimate exposure to the nature around them. Generations of wanderings told the nomadic peoples of the Great Plains where they were likely to find water in a summer drought, or how to dig in the sandy soil to find it. Thousands of years of experience informed them by position of sun and stars and shifts in the season when to expect the migrating bison herds to pass. Trial and error had taught them which wild berries and roots and even grasses were fit to eat, and which might have some medicinal – and even hallucinogenic and therefore mystical – properties.[2]

And even though the Europeans thought them primitive – as technologically they were – still the native peoples of North America had developed highly sophisticated social and cultural structures, all

Right: *A Cree Indian returning from a rabbit hunt reveals clothing that is both functional and decorative. Indians had to learn how to tan and cure the deerskin properly to make it soft, how to use sinew as thread to sew clothing together, and how to bend willow boughs without breaking them to make hoops for snowshoes.*

of which in their way encouraged survival. Just as in Europe, labor was divided between men and women. The women did the menial camp work, foraged for vegetables in the wild or – among the village building peoples – cultivated gardens, and raised the children. They skinned the kills from the hunt and made the clothing, and among nomads made the wigwams and teepees. Yet they also often held matriarchal rule inside the wigwam or Hogan, exercising considerable political authority on matters outside of hunting and war, the exclusive provinces of their men. It was a system that ensured enough importance to ensure women's survival in an environment that was otherwise so much a man's world.[3]

The men, meanwhile, sometimes specialized in their tasks, some making bows and arrows, others making knives or tomahawks, though just as often a warrior preferred to make his own, since his labor might imbue

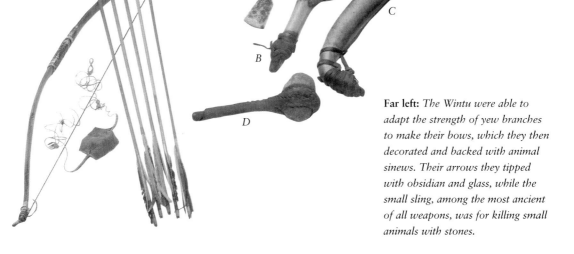

A

B

C

D

Below: *With the hunt accomplished, the work of Indian women only began. Crow women used these tools to render everything useful from an animal carcass. A and B are fleshers for scraping hides before tanning. C is an adze made from bone for chopping, while D is a maul used to crush bones to extract the marrow.*

Far left: *The Wintu were able to adapt the strength of yew branches to make their bows, which they then decorated and backed with animal sinews. Their arrows they tipped with obsidian and glass, while the small sling, among the most ancient of all weapons, was for killing small animals with stones.*

Right: *Two Yuma warriors used low-tension long bows and arrows without points, requiring them to get very close to their prey. Failing that, they relied on hardwood clubs to take the small game that flourished in their arid homeland.*

Far right: *Among the most skilled of all native hunters, these Apache used short bows but very long arrows, because they did their hunting on foot. To protect their feet in the hot desert, they wore moccasins more like boots. The headband, too, was more than decorative: in the desert it kept sweat from a hunter's eyes.*

Below: *The Pima in the Southwest carved war clubs from the gnarly mesquite tree. They were no match for the Spaniards, whom they first encountered in the 1690s. Accustomed to training their weapons on small game, they could hardly threaten steel armor and muskets.*

his weapon with his own special power. Among the woodland peoples the bows stretched to six feet or more, longer than their wielders were tall, and were so fashioned as to be light to carry without loss of strength, able to launch an arrow 300 feet or more with enough force to bring down a deer or a man. On the Plains, among the mounted warriors that appeared after the Spaniards introduced the horse in the 1500s, the bows were shorter to be more wieldy for use while riding. With practice, a warrior could fire several aimed arrows in the span of a minute, and in battle he alternately fired his own shafts and dodged and danced about trying to avoid those fired by his foes. One observer in the 1600s observed that it was through this "leaping and dancing, that seldom an arrow hits."

While lances were in the main more ceremonial than practical, a warrior always carried a club or tomahawk if possible, and indeed the word tomahawk came to describe all manner of weapons intended for bludgeoning, hacking, and the like. At the end of a long handle he might tie a large stone, or embed sharp seashells, or a

Left: *Of all the native peoples the whites encountered in the New World, probably the tribes making up the Iroquoian confederation excited the most interest and awe. This Mohawk warrior, shown as he would have appeared circa 1750, has adapted the New World to the Old, carrying an English Tower Flintlock musket, a French powder horn, and a steel-headed trade tomahawk, while wearing his ancient war clothes and knife.*

Above: *For many peoples, transportation represented the key to survival, a means of getting themselves to their food sources, or to meet their enemies. The Haida of the Northwest coast built elaborate canoes from hollowed-out red cedar trees, in which they braved the Pacific for seals and fish.*

honed stone, metal or even wooden spike. While it was surely lethal in hand-to-hand fighting, the tomahawk could also be thrown, and with practice some Indians could achieve deadly aim at distances reported to be up to forty yards.[4]

As swift as they could be on their feet, Indians all across the continent recognized the extra advantage that increased speed and mobility gave them. Virtually all adopted the horse as it spread from Mexico upward into the center of the continent and then toward the coasts. Virtually all developed means of turning willow boughs and other woods into frameworks and covering them with animal skins or tree bark to make canoes. Or they would hollow out logs to produce canoes and sometimes enormous dugout boats capable of carrying more than forty men and even of venturing some distance onto the oceans. Among those who lived in the northern climes, snowshoes appeared as manifestations of native ingenuity in overcoming an impediment of the elements.

Even more so than enemy tribes, the greatest threat to an aboriginal American was hunger and exposure. Thus, whether

Left: *In a land of abundance, and with few human enemies, some natives like the Pomo of northern California fished in reed boats, hunted in the redwood forests, and gathered what grew wild in a fertile eco-system.*

Below: *By contrast, the Ingelik near the Arctic, took ling cod by digging holes in the ice and then submerging traps, one of which this man is emptying. In an inhospitable land, they were dependent on their home-made tools, the harshness of the weather, and luck.*

traveling or living in long established villages, virtually all native peoples discovered some means of preserving foods for the journey or the long winters. They dried fish and bison and venison, or made pemmican from meats and grains and animal fat. They ground their maize into meal that they could eat dry on the journey, a single mouthful being sufficient to keep a warrior going for miles. In the winter they retained their body heat with layers of clothing and heavy robes of bison and bear skins, and in the summer stripped down to bare

Right: *A simple tool like the snowshoe could open whole regions to exploitation by native peoples. These Cree snowshoes used sinew or strips of buckskin to make the webbing inside wooden hoops. In the contest for game, these allowed natives to follow prey into the harshest environments.*

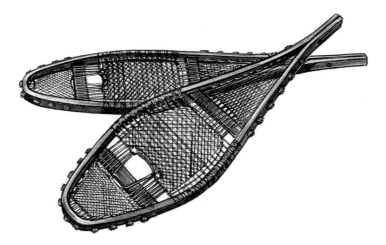

essentials to stay cool, with a lack of modesty that surprised whites whom they encountered.[5]

They also learned that as important was speed of movement, so was speed of communication, and especially in silence in the presence of danger. Thus they mastered the hoots and howls and chirps or a host of woodland and prairie creatures, sometimes their scouts actually being names for the animals they mimicked – the Bird, the Owl, the Fox, and so on. A set of signals could be communicated by a man silhouetted on a hillside to others a mile or more distant if the sun were right.

Of course, the much-vaunted – and misunderstood – smoke signal was also most useful, chiefly in the open country of the central prairies and Great Plains, where a fire made of damp brush could create enough dense smoke that a blanket thrown over it then removed, and thus repeated, could send a series of puffs skyward that might be visible more than fifty miles distant. The information communicated by such means was limited, but enough to warn of an approaching enemy, or summon war parties to concentrate on a foe, or locate a herd of bison.

All of this, though, required one more skill, and that was keen vision. Cooper did perhaps overdo his portrait of Indian eyesight, but numerous

Left: *Snowshoes could be very clumsy to walk in, yet the natives learned a shuffling sort of gait that actually allowed them considerable speed, while keeping them from simply burying themselves up to their knees. It also helped hunters like these Chippewa from freezing their feet.*

Below: *What the bison was to the Plains Indians, fish were to coastal and lake peoples, like these northwestern natives fishing with clubs and spears below Kettle Falls on the Columbia River. The fat salmon were taken as they swam upstream at Spokane, Colville, Walla Walla, and elsewhere, on their way to spawning grounds.*

white witnesses testified to the natives' wonderful vision. "I have good 'plains eyes,'" boasted Colonel Richard Dodge of the United States Army in the late 1800s, "but while, even with an excellent field glass, I could scarcely make out that a distant speck was a horseman, the Indian by my side would tell me what the distant speck was saying."[6]

Colonel Dodge was hyperbolic perhaps, but still it was admiring testimony from a former foe to the kinds of skills that enabled the native peoples of North America to survive until their way of life was all but ground to dust by the weight of technology and organization.

CHAPTER TWO

The First European Arrivals

"Thousands of years of cultural development were rudely diverted and truncated by the arrival of Europeans."
(Colin F. Taylor in "The Native Americans," referring to the Southeast tribes)

O N JUNE 24, 1521, Pedro de Quejo, piloting a Spanish caravel out of Cuba, sighted land on the coast of what is today South Carolina. Some hours later he and others rowed ashore where almost immediately they met a group of curious natives whose tribal name does not survive, though later legend called them the Chicora. The Indians swarmed the shore to get a look at this new apparition on their firmament, but as soon as the Europeans stepped off their boats the natives ran away in fear. The Spaniards chased them, caught a man and woman, and forced them back to the boats. There the

Right: *When the first Europeans arrived in the Southwest, they encountered ancient peoples who hundreds of years before had developed means of building and surviving in communities like the pueblo at Conchiti, which dated back to the thirteenth century at least.*

Spaniards gave them gifts and dressed them in their own clothes, then attempted through gestures and signs to convince the frightened aboriginals that they came as friends. That done, they released them to return to their tribe in the hope that these ersatz emissaries would convince the others to come. It worked, and soon many of the Indians went to their home in the interior wearing shirts and caps and neckerchiefs, persuading their chief to send gifts of food in return.

In that episode Quejo and his companions showed that they had well learned an essential survival skill that came out of the previous generation of the first European encounters with the natives of this strange land. When outnumbered by hundreds to one, even Spanish steel and matchlocks were no match. The best chance of survival lay in making and maintaining friendly relations with the inhabitants, even if it required bribes in the form of gifts of cheap trinkets and beads.[1]

Unfortunately, such good relations – when made – usually broke down all too soon, especially when the exploitative motives of the Europeans became apparent to the natives. Quejo's own expedition was bent in the end on taking Indians back to Cuba as slaves to work Spanish mines. When that happened, the gifts and open hand policy stood little chance of continuing to work. Not only did that mean the Europeans now had to worry about survival against native reprisals, but also that they could no longer count on bartering gifts for food. They either had to take it by force, import their own from home at great cost and hazard, or else begin to provide locally for themselves. The same was true of the information they needed on geography and terrain, where to find good water and game, mountain passes, animal trails, and more.

So long as relations with natives were good, these interlopers

Above: *When whites arrived in North America, they could not at first have survived without the native peoples, either by exploitation, or friendly trade, and at first most of the Indians were amenable, if guarded. Jamestown, Plymouth, and other first settlements would have foundered but for native assistance.*

could survive in fair degree and live as they had in the Old World, building their European-style shelters and "buying" what they needed otherwise. It was in the breakdown of relations with the Indians that the Spaniards – and the French and English, and even much later Russians – were forced to learn for themselves essential skills to survive thousands of miles from home in a hostile environment.

It was an environment almost totally foreign to the previous experience even of the most traveled European. By the late fifteenth century, most of these men came from families of farmers, coastal fishermen, or city dwellers. In Spain, France, and England, very few had to feed themselves meat and grain by their own devices except for farmers. The same men might also have a little experience in trapping vermin, and surely most had some exposure to leisure fishing in fresh water. But only upper class grandees and noblemen – of whom few came to the New World – had known either the leisure time or the opportunity to hunt game, and even they still really knew little at all about stalking and following a trail.

They had no knowledge at all of native plants in the New World, as to which were edible, which medicinal, and which deadly. As the ensuing decades would demonstrate to them, the weather in North America was the most violent and changeable in the world. What should they do in a hurricane? Earthquakes, at least, were known to some of them, but what was a tornado? How should they build their dwellings, and of what, in order to withstand such elements? The heat and humidity of summer could be stifling, but men from Mediterranean climates had some experience in handling that. But what about the unseen and unknown fevers and miasmas awaiting them in the dense woods and swamps?

The Spanish exploiters

These hazards and more confronted all of the European peoples who came to North America and ventured west of the Mississippi River. Different cultures met them in different ways. The Spaniards were the earliest, the most settled in their Old World ways, and, because their motivation for centuries was chiefly exploitation rather than

Left: *"The Mission San Gabriel," painted in 1832 by Ferdinand Deppe, was a part of the "string of pearls" that Juniperro Serra built in California to bring European religion to the natives, and at the same time provide a focus for Spaniards' catholic faith. In time the missions became essential centers of both Spanish and Indian community.*

settlement, they also showed the least inclination to adapt. They came to conquer, to make fortunes if they could, and then take their new wealth back to their old homes. To be sure, many wound up remaining permanently in the new land, but even the passage of centuries saw little change in their habits. Their society remained highly stratified, not for survival, but out of ancient habit. At the top stood the *peninsulares*, men actually born in Spain, the men who ruled. Next came the *creoles*, men of pure Spanish blood who were born in the New World. Then came the *mestizos*, the half-breed offspring of Spaniards and natives, and then at the bottom were the Indians themselves.

The *peninsulares* and *creoles* took few pains to educate themselves on survival. For that they depended instead on their social position, their wealth, the force of their arms, and their control of the Catholic Church in the New World. The weight of all these allowed the upper classes to compel their social inferiors to do the hard work of surviving for them. Both collectively and individually, survival for the *peninsulares* and *creoles* depended more than anything else on subjugation.

The Indian tribes in their proximity posed little or no threat because the Spaniards either dispersed them or made them slaves,

27

using the twin weapons of the sword and the cross to keep them docile. Indeed, slavery, of the native peoples at first and later of Africans, would be the driving engine of Spanish civilization in North America until 1821, when the successful Mexican revolution finally ousted the Spaniards from the mainland and abolished their slavery of the Indians. What still remained, however, was the ancient system of *peonage* that made virtual serfs of the Indians and even the *mestizos*. It was an ordered society that depended upon that order for the survival of the many, and for the benefit of the few. Only that few raised the crops, tended the livestock, composed the levies of *soldados* raised for defense, and they far more than any of the upper classes, learned to mimic the outdoor survival skills to be learned from the native peoples themselves.

Early on, the Spaniards did try diplomacy, especially the farther into the continent they penetrated as their advance left them more exposed, and farther from their bases on the seacoasts. By the late 1700s Spain had established peaceful relations through gifts and trade – and intimidation where required – with tribes as far north as the border with Canada, and westward onto the Great Plains, at the same time extending settlement with missions and *presidios*, and consequent domination of the largely docile coastal tribes, all the way up California to some distance north of San Francisco Bay.[2] In time they got to understand that it was easier to learn enough of tribal customs and superstitions to use them rather than muskets and swords to achieve their ends. Most of the native peoples had a highly developed sense of ceremony and ritual, and Spanish explorers, soldiers, and

Below: *The Spaniards were not unduly sympathetic to the conquered peoples of the Southwest, and those not overwhelmed were often expelled. Others fled, like the Zuni who recoiled from turmoil with Franciscan priests, and withdrew to an eyrie atop Taaiyalone Mesa, seen in the distance, where they tried to avoid contact.*

frontiersmen learned to behave with due solemnity even on mundane occasions, and in the native languages if possible. Special symbolic gifts of medals and necklaces, even Spanish flags, became especially useful.[3]

There was also craft and guile in such ceremonial gifts, for the Spanish early realized – as did the other Europeans that followed – that they could make their own position more secure by capitalizing on ancient tribal rivalries among the natives, and even intra-tribal dissension. Recognizing only a few chiefs within any given tribe with gifts and ceremony naturally aroused jealousy among other chiefs not so recognized. The result was the weakening of that tribe as a potential threat to the Spaniards while the chiefs and their aligned warriors were distracted by their own factional disputes. On a grander scale, an alliance with one tribe could take advantage of that group's hostility toward another tribe and end up in having both groups expending their energy and blood against each other rather than directing it at the Europeans.[4] In its simplest reduction, it was "divide and conquer," a survival technique as old as civilization.

Left: *Europeans coming to the New World did not as a rule have to worry about technological competition. Indians could be a threat, but their weapons, like the leather shield carried by this Navajo war captain, were no match for bullets.*

Below: *The whites never conquered some of the native peoples, particularly the Seminoles, an offshoot of the Creek nation that merged with other tribes in the woods and swamps of central Florida. They would fight two wars with the later United States, and emerge unbeaten from both.*

The French explorers

Interestingly, in their efforts at diplomacy with the internal tribes of the Mississippi Valley, the Spaniards borrowed a page from the book of the French, whose approach to survival in North America was otherwise dramatically opposite to that of the Iberians.[5] Where the Spaniards made little effort to assimilate to achieve survival, the French who came to these shores went farther than any others. Like the Spaniards, the French were indefatigable explorers, and even

Above: *The wisest settlers and explorers made it their business to get along amicably with the native peoples. Captain John Smith of the first Jamestown, Virginia, colony, is shown in this illustration bartering goods for Indian corn. Smith would use both trade and muskets to achieve his ends with the Indians.*

Above right: *Those who came to make new homes very quickly set about the work of agriculture, and if they were smart they learned from the Indians to grow the local native fruits and vegetables, like these pumpkins and potatoes and other things in front of a settler's cabin at Jamestown.*

more so mapmakers. They took pains to learn the geography of their new environment, its hazards and advantages. Thanks to their early and much more pacific policy toward the native peoples, they learned from them where to expect to find water and game in the unknown interior, and how the seasons affected certain prairies and savannahs.

While it was true that many of the French came for quick exploitation, many more came to make new homes, and thus they took pains to learn the survival ways of their Indian neighbors and allies. Within a generation or two they were adopting Indian clothing, learning their ways in the hunt and on a long trek, their ways of preserving food, and their knowledge of roots and herbs. Even before 1700, as the French penetrated the Mississippi Valley in what became the Louisiana Territory, they were studying the migration of the bison on the prairies, or learning the cultivation of pumpkins and corn from the peoples along the Illinois River.

As the French spread westward across Canada, they became ever more assimilated, frequently marrying into native tribes both to make alliances for protection as well as to start families. They built Indian canoes and dugouts, learned to trap for furs, and accommodated themselves to their environment rather than, as with the Spanish, trying simply to dominate it.[6] It is hardly a surprise that when the time for a great war for empire came in North America in 1756, the native peoples overwhelmingly sided with the French against the British.

The Russian foothold

More than a thousand miles west from the outposts of the French Canadian *voyageurs*, another European culture with dramatic differences came to make a foothold on the north Pacific coast and face rather different challenges to survival. Late in the 1700s Russians began to turn their eyes eastward from Siberia. It was but a brief journey across the Bering Strait – crossable on foot sometimes over frozen water – to Alaska. Much of the Strait was seemingly uninhabitable, and yet the Eskimo and Aleut and other tribes eked out a life, and by adopting their heavy winter clothing, especially by learning their means of survival in the coldest temperatures, the Russians could gain access to the riches of the streams and lakes in the abundance of fur-bearing creatures. Land farther south on the coast was more temperate, and in the early 1800s the Russians established themselves at Fort Ross and elsewhere less than 100 miles north of San Francisco. They became neighbors to both the native tribes and the Spaniards.

It was a precarious outpost, and one doomed eventually to commercial failure and abandonment, but there, perched on the cliffs above the Pacific, the Russians tried to insert a European community into a stockade in the wilderness. For them, survival meant bringing from home almost all they needed but game and fish. Amid a largely peaceful and sparse native population, they had little fear of hostilities, and instead simply traded with the natives for the pelts that brought wealth. Established as merchants and middlemen between Indians and markets at home, they had little need to adapt, and so barely tried. The only real challenge to their survival was the market in Europe and at home for furs. And when that declined they disappeared, just as another set of white explorers and settlers were on the way who would eclipse the dominion of all the other Europeans who invaded the West, and who would face the briefest, and yet perhaps most severe, challenges to survival of them all.

Above: *On the faraway Pacific coast settlers of another kind had to learn to cope with the cold, the isolation, and the natives. Russian fur traders established Fort Ross in northern California and learned to rely heavily on the natives to supply them by trade with what they needed to survive.*

CHAPTER THREE

The Explorers

"It satisfied desire and it created desire, the desire of the westering nation."
(Bernard Devoto on Lewis and Clark's report of their
Corps of Discovery expedition)

SOMEWHERE in between the Spanish and the French approaches to surviving on the new continent came that of the British and their later independent American descendants. While not as harsh or exploitative as the former, the Anglos still never quite "went native" to the degree of the latter. They also enjoyed some unique advantages. By being latecomers to the West, they had the benefit of almost two centuries of prior French and Spanish experience and exploration. They would encounter Indian peoples who already knew the white man, and in the Louisiana Territory the bulk of those relations had been with the more peaceful French, who left the English Americans a predominant legacy of tolerance and limited good will among the Indians. There would be hostilities aplenty ahead, of course, but those would largely be of the English-speaking settlers' own making. Moreover, as the Americans came and Anglo settlement jumped across the Mississippi early in the 1800s and began advancing westward, they had already had more than enough experience from their encounters with the woodland native peoples to the east to help them survive while learning native practices peculiar to the new land ahead. Thus, more than any Europeans in the West before them, they were ready for the challenges awaiting them on the doorstep of a new western empire.

MAP AS AT 1810 TERRITORY

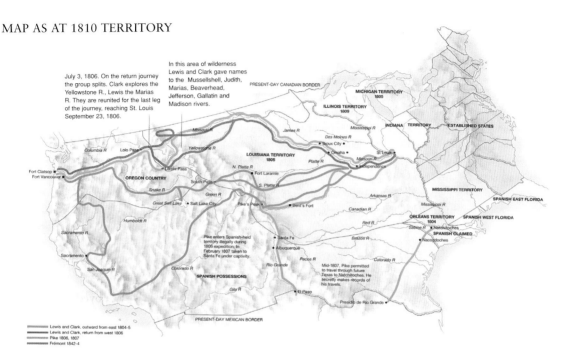

July 3, 1806. On the return journey the group splits. Clark explores the Yellowstone R., Lewis the Marias R. They are reunited for the last leg of the journey, reaching St. Louis September 23, 1806.

In this area of wilderness Lewis and Clark gave names to the Mussellshell, Judith, Marias, Beaverhead, Jefferson, Gallatin and Madison rivers.

PRESENT-DAY CANADIAN BORDER

MICHIGAN TERRITORY 1805

ILLINOIS TERRITORY 1809

INDIANA TERRITORY

ESTABLISHED STATES

Missouri R

James R

Des Moines R

Mississippi R

Columbia R

Sioux City

Omaha

Lolo Pass

Yellowstone R

LOUISIANA TERRITORY 1805

Platte R

St. Louis

Missouri R

Lemhi Pass

N. Platte R

Fort Laramie

Independence

Fort Clatsop
Fort Vancouver

OREGON COUNTRY

South Pass

S. Platte R

Snake R

Green R

Arkansas R

MISSISSIPPI TERRITORY

SPANISH EAST FLORIDA

Great Salt Lake

Salt Lake City

Pike's Peak

Bent's Fort

Canadian R

Mississippi R

ORLEANS TERRITORY 1804

SPANISH WEST FLORIDA

Humboldt R

Red R

Sabine R

Natchitoches

SPANISH CLAIMED

Sacramento R

Santa Fe

Brazos R

Nacogdoches

Sacramento

Albuquerque

Pecos R

Colorado R

Pike enters Spanish-held territory illegally during 1806 expedition. In February 1807 taken to Santa Fe under captivity.

Rio Grande

Mid-1807, Pike permitted to travel through future Texas to Natchitoches. He secretly makes records of his travels.

San Joaquin R

Colorado R

SPANISH POSSESSIONS

Gila R

El Paso

Presidio de Rio Grande

PRESENT-DAY MEXICAN BORDER

Lewis and Clark, outward from east 1804-5
Lewis and Clark, return from west 1806
Pike 1806, 1807
Frémont 1842-4

Above: *European peoples found a host of ways to spread themselves westward once they crossed the Mississippi, and from a multiplicity of motivations. The purchase of the vast Louisiana Territory in 1803 made the United States a continental power over a largely unknown territory. But there were hopes of trade routes to the West, of tapping the commerce of the Pacific, as well as a need to protect a northern border with former and future foe Great Britain. Fortunes could be made in furs and perhaps in the natural and mineral riches of the interior. Explorers Lewis and Clark made the first epic examination of just a part of the Purchase, taking almost four years to cross the continent from St. Louis through latter day Omaha and Sioux City, along the track of the Missouri and Yellowstone Rivers, to the mouth of the Columbia River at Fort Clatsop. The trails they left behind were the origin of later highways of settlement, especially the Oregon and California Trails that took settlers from Independence, Missouri, across Kansas and Nebraska to Colorado, then across the Rocky Mountains and the deserts of Utah and Nevada, to follow the Columbia to the Pacific, or down the Sierras to California. Meanwhile the Santa Fe Trail that opened the Southwest fur trade appeared at the same time, going from Independence across Kansas and then south along the fringe of Rocky foothills to trade with the Spaniards.*

Right: *Meriwether Lewis commanded the Corps of Discovery that explored the Louisiana Purchase. He survived natives, elements, exposure, hunger, and more, only to succumb to his own madness when he committed suicide three years later.*

Far right: *William Clark served as Lewis's second-in-command, and bore the rigors of the journey with more equanimity. Both proved adept at surviving by being adaptable and willing to learn from natives and* voyageurs *who had knowledge of the region already.*

Below: *Men venturing into the wilderness to explore and establish relations with the natives had to bring trade goods of some interest and value. The Indians wanted guns, to be sure, and thousands of English trade muskets like this .50 caliber smoothbore were brought west for them, along with glass beads, bone hair "pipes," and amber amulets.*

The Lewis and Clark expedition

The first dramatic test of their readiness came just at the dawn of the century that would see the United States rise to become a world power. In 1803 President Thomas Jefferson managed to purchase from Napoleon's France the vast Louisiana Territory, virtually half of the still unsettled continent west of the Mississippi. The problem was that he knew little or nothing about what he had bought. Thus in 1804 he sent his private secretary Meriwether Lewis and William Clark on an epic exploration with a "Corps of Discovery" to investigate the territory, especially with an eye to finding commercial water routes, if any, to the Pacific. The story of their 4,000 mile, two-and-one-half year journey, would become the stuff of legend, of novel and film and epic chronicle. Perhaps more amazing than their expedition's achievements themselves, however, is the fact that of the party of forty-four men who left St. Louis in the spring of 1804, only

one died on the journey. More amazing still, they had not one single hostile brush with the score of Indian tribes they met along the way. The entire trek was a lesson – an amazingly successful lesson – in frontier survival.

Following their own past experience, and that of both French and Spanish, Lewis and Clark took an abundance of trade goods with them as gifts for native peoples as encountered. Knowing the value of understanding aboriginal languages, they also took interpreters with them – though their usefulness would be increasingly limited the farther west the explorers went. Apart from being valuable for exchanging for necessary supplies, the trade goods were also carried as examples of the sort of items that might have commercial value in the East.

The explorers took along a sextant, a chronometer, and a spirit level, with all of which they could fix their daily positions and those of geographic features, and thus begin to fill in the vast blank void on the map of the West. Not only was this last important information for its own sake, but it also ensured that once they reached the Pacific and started back, they would have their own guide to retracing their steps, probably the first substantial use of terrestrial navigation as a survival skill on the frontier.

The individual instances in which Lewis and Clark made wise decisions affecting their Corps' survival are many. The most famous, of course, was their hiring of the French *voyageur* Toussaint Charbonneau as a guide. While of some use himself, his real worth came in his Shoshone wife Sacagawea, who would repeatedly intercede with the peoples they later encountered, especially her own tribe, at critical moments. Clark called her simply "our Indian woman," but she was a godsend. She showed them how to gather wild licorice on hillsides, where to find the breadroot sometimes called "white apples" that the Indians baked and mashed, how to dig in the earth to find wild Jerusalem artichokes and what the natives called "hog peanuts."[1] She knew something of native remedies to help the explorers, who on their journey had to face rheumatism, dysentery, abscesses and boils, scurvy, broken bones, fevers of all variety, infections, and even venereal diseases. Fortunately, the whites

brought along some of their own civilization's medicinal survival nostrums, though many were just as much based on superstition and ignorance, and even less effective, than native remedies. But they did have the opiate laudanum to help with pain, emetics, zinc sulphate to relieve sore eyes, saltpeter to combat fever, and even patent remedies from the East, like Rush's Pills to relieve constipation.[2]

For the more martial means of survival, the Corps left St. Louis armed with the new Model 1803 flintlock rifle, one of the first manufactured by the United States government at its own arsenal at Harpers Ferry, Virginia. It was vastly superior to the muskets that until recently had equipped the American military, its rifled .54 bore giving Lewis such a feeling of confidence that when he was exploring fauna he found that "I most generally went alone armed with my rifle" even in the known haunts of bears. At the same time, these men learned prudence. Once Lewis found himself being chased by a large bear and, when he turned to shoot the animal, remembered that he had not reloaded his rifle after last shooting it. Once extricated from the predicament, he resolved never to wait again between firing and reloading, so as always to be ready. Preparedness was the soul of survival.[3]

Opposite: *Essential to learning to survive in the wilderness was becoming familiar with the wild roots and berries, fruits and vegetables, that grew in the woods and prairies. Accommodating Indians, like this Quantsino woman picking salmonberries, showed the explorers what was fit to eat and what could be poisonous.*

Below: *One of the most beautiful military firearms ever manufactured, the Harpers Ferry 1803 .54 caliber flintlock rifle was the weapon that armed most of the Corps of Discovery. It was hardy, simple, and reliable, and was also the first military longarm designed and manufactured by the United States.*

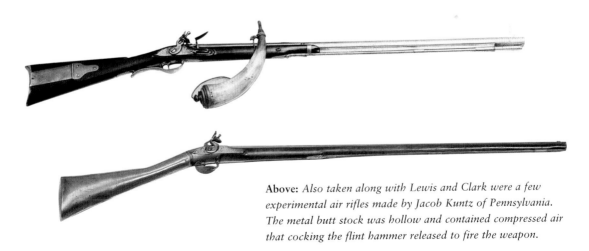

Above: *Also taken along with Lewis and Clark were a few experimental air rifles made by Jacob Kuntz of Pennsylvania. The metal butt stock was hollow and contained compressed air that cocking the flint hammer released to fire the weapon.*

Toward that same end the explorers learned not to be profligate or careless with their supplies and equipment. Even Sacagawea got a reprimand for gorging herself on dried fish. Feasting to excess was characteristic of many Indian tribes, who might eat gluttonously until ill after a fresh kill, and then go hungry for days afterward until the next meat was taken. Their imperfect means of preserving of food in part encouraged such gorging, though it was also the natural practice of almost all predators in the wild. But Lewis and Clark had to think ahead. Nomadic or pastoral peoples could lay at rest for days after a feast, needing little nourishment, but the Corps of Discovery had to work hard and move on every day in good weather, which required a steady diet. Virtually all whites who followed in their footsteps would do the same. Those who did not more often than not fell victims of their own folly. This extended to keeping the men's moccasins mended and in good repair, their guns well oiled, their powder dry. To be sure, more than once they would approach starvation in a hard winter, but careful planning and cool heads – as well as luck – saw them through.[4]

Zebulon Pike's quest

While the expedition by Lewis and Clark served as a template and model for subsequent survival challenges by future exploring parties, none ever matched it for its spectacular success. Just as the Corps of Discovery was returning to St. Louis, Washington sent Lieutenant Zebulon Pike to lead a party to explore the area of the Great Plains west to the Rocky Mountains and to the sources of the Red and Arkansas Rivers. Though his mission was in part a failure – Pike never found the river sources, mistakenly identified a great desert where there was none, and was finally captured by Spanish soldiers out of Santa Fe – the lieutenant still discovered much. His trek, however, was more a raid for information than a quest for learning, his survival dependent – as long as it lasted – on speed and that other essential ingredient to be found in Lewis and Clark and in all who successfully followed them west, endurance. Perhaps more than any other quality of character, it required an unwillingness to give up, a determination to persevere, to survive out there.[5]

Opposite: Celebrated Western artist Charles M. Russell created this stirring, if romanticized, painting of "Lewis and Clark on the Lower Columbia" in 1905. Still, it reveals how the explorers "went native" by adopting buckskin clothing and learning how to make dugout canoes.

Above: *Following in the explorers'
footsteps, settlers went west with
their essential supplies, sometimes
proclaiming their determination on
their wagons, just as these
excursionists have painted "Pike's
Peak or Bust 1860" on this wagon.*

Not long after Pike came another, more prudent exploration
under the command of Major Stephen H. Long. In 1819 he led an
expedition up the Missouri into present-day Nebraska, then set out
overland toward the Rockies to survey the Great Plains, map the
mountains, and find the source of the Red River. Major Long
committed his share of bumbles and misjudgments, but produced
out of it the best and most complete map to that time of the interior
of the Louisiana Territory, itself an essential survival tool for all who
would follow. While the native peoples committed the landscape to
their memory, but seldom migrated outside long-established routes
and hunting grounds, the whites forever sought to go where they
had not been, and in territory where they had no recollection to
guide them these maps and others to follow were essential. As the
history of the frontier progressed, the maps only became better, the
blank spaces fewer, the accuracy more acute.[6]

The formidable Jedediah Smith

Meanwhile, as the large expeditions fitted out and conducted by the government in Washington mapped and explored, there were intrepid and resourceful individuals who did much the same thing, largely to suit their own ends. They could not depend upon numbers for their safety in the wild. They did not have guides and interpreters or the latest in government equipment. Rather, they survived by their wits and ingenuity, motivated by curiosity and a fever for exploration, as well as by the promise of prosperity. Most notable among these early individualists was Jedediah Smith, who in September 1823 demonstrated his hardihood and determination by surviving an encounter with a bear that ripped away most of his scalp and tore off one of his ears. Smith himself, in extreme pain, gave companions directions on how to sew his scalp and ear back into place, and within ten days he was back on the trail again. Before long, after enduring a brutal winter of blizzards and near starvation, Smith – following hints given him by Crow Indians – passed over the Continental Divide through what later became known as South Pass, and thus opened the way through the mountains that would be followed by a generation of immigrants.

Not content with that, he would later find another pass opening the way to the great Salt Lake, and in 1827 would find a route through the Sierra Mountains to become the first known white man to reach California overland. In the process he discovered that in the desert he could stay alive through the heat by burying himself in the sand during the day. Surprised and attacked by Mojave Indians, he

Below: *The workhorse survival tool for whites from earliest frontier days until the 1840s was the flintlock rifle, which appeared in a host of varieties. This one has two firing pans and barrels, and after one is fired, the over-and-under barrels are simply twisted to bring another barrel in line ready to fire.*

Left: *Jedediah Smith survived by his wits, and in the process opened much of the Southwest, but even an experienced frontiersman like him could be careless or caught unawares. Mohave braves like this one caught him, ending his career at the ends of their mesquite war clubs, knives, and lances. Loyalties and allegiances could shift quickly and dramatically. Not long before they killed him, the Mohaves had been trading with him.*

resorted to a stratagem based on understanding of the natives' desire more for goods than scalps, and diverted them by spreading his trade goods out on the ground along a stream, and expecting that when his attackers stopped to reap the bounty he could make his escape. But even a man as seasoned as Smith could suddenly find himself taking one risk too many. In 1831, while scouting for water on the Santa Fe trail, he met a party of mounted Comanche who took him by surprise and with bullets and lances ended his extraordinary career.[7]

Smith and several more of his ilk – James Bridger, Christopher "Kit" Carson, William Sublette, William "Old Bill" Williams – survived incredible hardships and dangers through their wits, what they had learned, and sometimes just the raw determination to live. Hugh Glass, one of the most bold and reckless of them all, walked into a thicket in the Yellowstone country west of the Missouri River, and ran smack into a female grizzly bear and her cubs. In a protective rage, the bear leapt upon Glass as he shot her with his rifle. As he tried to climb a tree to safety, the animal pulled him down and raked his whole body with its claws before it fell dead atop him. Glass's companions found him torn and shredded from his scalp to his thighs, with his throat punctured and blood pouring forth. Hopeless as he appeared, the others tried for a time to carry him to safety from hostile Arikara Indians in the neighborhood, but soon they simply abandoned him for a doomed man. But Hugh Glass had other ideas. Unable to walk, he crawled, spending six weeks in the wilderness living on berries, insects, the occasional snake, and even rotting bison carcasses. He covered some 200 miles at five miles a day until he reached Fort Kiowa, there to recuperate until he was well enough to seek vengeance on the men who abandoned him. There was the ultimate skill that characterized all who combated the wilderness and survived, the simple refusal to give up.[8]

Left: *Among the most famous of all Mountain Men, and most adept at survival, was Jim Bridger. He spent seventeen years in the wilderness, opened new trails, survived harrowing dangers, and became known as the "King of the Mountain Men."*

Left: *Christopher "Kit" Carson achieved notoriety as a Mountain Man and trapper, then as a guide for the explorations of John C. Frémont, and later as a brigadier general in the Union Army during the Civil War. He also became the first real celebrity man of the wilderness.*

43

CHAPTER FOUR

The Mountain Men

*"He was a survival specialist in the face of bitterly cold winters,
antagonistic Indians, and unbelievably powerful bears."*
(George Laycock in the preface to his book, "The Mountain Men")

THERE WAS PERHAPS something contradictory in the very name that attached itself to those who came to be known as Mountain Men. Mountains stand in ranges, side by side in their scores or even hundreds. The Mountain Men, on the other hand, often spent their real working time isolated or in pairs as they set and harvested their traps, vulnerable prey to watchful native parties. Contrary to popular misconception, however, the Mountain Man did not spend his life in near-total isolation. Even in their heyday in the 1820s and 1830s, before the demand for beaver pelts died and with it their way of life, there were probably never more than 1,000 of them, and they were no fools.[1] They knew how vulnerable the single man was in a hostile environment, and not only to attack by native raiders, but to the elements too, and to the possibility of sickness and injury.

In fact, when roving the streams and valleys of the Rocky Mountains, they usually traveled in substantial groups that they called "brigades," sometimes numbering up to sixty or more, for mutual protection. Armed with their black powder rifles and pistols, even a dozen or so trappers could feel relatively secure that they could defend themselves against several times their number of natives, few of whom were yet equipped with firearms. Nor were they exposed to the elements or to hostile warriors all year round. They hunted and trapped only in the spring and fall, when the beaver were most plentiful and full grown. The cold months they spent in a

stationary winter quarters, while in the summer they met at Taos, Mexico, and Jackson Hole, Wyoming, and elsewhere for the annual rendezvous that brought hundreds together to sell furs, drink and frolic, spend what little they received for their pelts, and run up sufficient debts with sutlers outfitting themselves for the next season that they had no choice but to go out and trap again.

A loose cultural homogeneity helped them withstand the dangers ahead. Despite the fact that the best remembered of them bore Anglo names like Bill Williams and Kit Carson, the overwhelming majority of them bore French Canadian blood, and tended to band together in their brigades, making the Americans, Spaniards, and the few free blacks feel somewhat like outsiders. Moreover, regardless of the ethnic caste of a brigade, there were certain social strata within it – as within the whole Mountain Man enterprise – that encouraged survival while at the same time perpetuating a hierarchy.

Above: *French and Indian voyageurs exploited the northern rivers of America for generations, and wisely the Europeans made peaceful relations with the native peoples, intermarrying with them, in the quest for furs and fortune, like this boatload of mixed native and white voyageurs in Ontario in 1860.*

Left: *The* voyageur *adopted the Indian bark canoe, yet kept a rigidly stratified society just as did the Mountain Men, the hunters and trappers standing far above the mere rowers. Theirs was one of the kinds of social organizations emphasizing specialization that helped all survive.*

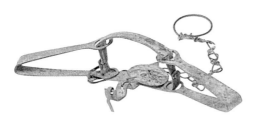

At the bottom of the ladder in Mountain Man society were the "pork eaters," new men to the mountains, working for the trapping companies and paid only their salaries. They were not allowed traps and the chance to take furs for themselves, but given only the menial camp tasks while they watched and learned from more experienced men. Above them were the trappers who were actually employed by the companies, part of their task being to hunt for and feed the trappers and also to run traps for their employers. But at least they got a salary and actually fared better than many of the independent men who had to bargain and negotiate when they sold pelts. Then there came the men who were not paid by a company, but who were outfitted and equipped by one, and were thus indebted, and had to trap enough pelts to pay off that indebtedness before they made anything for themselves. They seldom, if ever, got out of debt, but at least they were free from all of the camp and hunting chores, and thus stood apart from the rest.[2]

At the top of the profession was the independent trapper, a man working exclusively for himself, not indebted to any supplier and not necessarily contracted to any firm like the Hudson's Bay Company. He could go where he would, and buy from and sell to whomever he chose. Of them all he was the most likely to operate on his own, or with a very small group of associates, while the "company" men more often brigaded. He was likely the most boastful and "larger than life," more extravagant in his spending and spreeing, and more reckless in the wild. Perhaps not surprisingly, those who survived honed exceptional individual skills, yet even these men, when careless or complacent enough to be caught alone or unawares, like Bill Williams

Above: *Bent's Fort was erected on the Arkansas River in Colorado in 1823, a combination of pueblo architecture and Old World fortification. The trappers needed places where they could "hole up" for the winter, as well as take refuge from occasional Indian hostilities.*

when the Utes surrounded him in 1849, faced a brutal death.[3]

The salient point to the stratification of Mountain Man society was that at all levels, even the most menial, it encouraged specialization through experience, and that worked toward improving the survival expectations of all. The man who started as a "pork eater" and worked his way up through the ranks to contract or independent trapping was thus a man steeped in experience by a virtual apprenticeship of necessity. In the wild, when actually on the hunt for pelts, the Mountain Men traveled from valley to valley in their brigades, and broke off singly and in groups of two or more only when they spread along streams to lay out their traps, for each man's traps were his own and the catch his to pay his debts and – with luck – fill his purse. That is when they were in most danger from attack, but as soon as the traps were laid or the beaver taken and the traps taken up again, they returned to brigade camp. Usually they located those camps on some high place allowing a good view to prevent their being surprised, and on terrain that afforded some measure of natural protection. If the brigade expected to spend

Left: *The Mountain Man was something of a marvel of adaptation in the interest of survival. He carried the latest in weaponry, like the percussion cap-and-ball rifle shown here, yet he dressed almost entirely in the Indian manner, a combination of camouflage and practicality.*

several days or weeks operating from a base camp, the pork eaters were put to work building some rude defenses as a precaution.

Weapons and tactics

When forced to fight for his life, the Mountain Man's experience – especially that of the hunters and independent trappers who used their rifles frequently – served him well. He carried a superior weapon to any in the hands of Indian attackers. Since he was almost always on the defensive when he had to fight, he could choose his ground and make the foe come to him. He had learned more than enough from hunting – if not from those very same Indians – to know the arts of concealment. At the same time, the brigades had men in command who could direct fire and even volleys if necessary, though most threats to a brigade camp were isolated attempts to cut out a horse or two.

Furthermore, most brigades were large enough to deter attack by small roving parties of Indians. Perhaps the only "battle" actually

Below: *The Mountain Men often borrowed transportational ideas from the natives, such as this travois, nothing more than a triangular arrangement of lodge poles fixed behind a horse, and on which hundreds of pounds of gear could be loaded, as well as furs, a sick or wounded comrade, and the like.*

fought by a brigade involved around fifty company men and independent trappers and some 200 Gros Ventre Indians at Pierre's Hole (in modern Wyoming) in July 1832. It began with the trappers taking a Gros Ventre leader by surprise and killing him as he was shaking hands. Surprise – even by deceit – was a survival skill used by white and native alike. The trappers then proceeded sporadically to attack as the reluctant natives took refuge in nearby underbrush. In the action it was very much every man for himself. "We do not marshall our forces, nor approach the scene of conflict in any regular order," recalled one trapper in a letter he actually wrote just afterward. "Each person goes 'on his own hook'."[4] If attackers caught him out in the open "on his own hook," however, even his rifle was of little avail if he faced enough attackers to simply overrun him, as probably happened with Williams.

Learning the languages

The real survival skills, however, were not so much those learned in battle, but those gained by less hazardous experience. Nothing served the Mountain Man's life expectancy better than learning the elements of the native languages. Few became fluent, perhaps, but virtually all learned enough to ask directions, bargain for food, or explain a misunderstanding short of violence, all of them passive efforts that could and did save their lives several times over. Inevitably, either singly or in small groups, the trappers and hunters found themselves confronted by armed native men with whom the wrong word or a misunderstood intention could bring sudden death. Language also helped Mountain Men form informal alliances with some tribes, taking advantage of inter-tribal feuds and rivalries, for their own ends, as when Flathead and Nez Perce warriors cooperated in attacks on the Gros Ventres at Pierre's Hole. From the Indians they also adopted clothing and appearance, so much so that to tell a Mountain Man that he had been mistaken for an Indian was considered a high compliment.[5]

Thanks in part to what he gleaned from natives, as well as his own travels and observations, Warren Ferris, an employee of fur outfit B. Pratte & Company and who had spent five years in the mountains as

Right: *The Indians, too, could adapt in their struggle to keep up with the white man in survival techniques. Where the native gave the whites clothing and trail lore, the whites could provide men like this Nez Perce warrior a Henry "Yellow Boy" repeating rifle to augment his bow and arrows.*

a trapper, was able to produce a map of the mountains and rivers to guide him.[6] Most Mountain Men learned the Indian trails and the bison trails, the location of the vital passes, the courses of the streams, where the water holes lay, and how to read the signs of beaver activity. Then the men themselves moved as much as possible in the water to avoid leaving their smell on the ground to frighten the animals. They set their traps below the surface, and baited them overhead with scent smeared on from other beavers' sexual glands.

The successful Mountain Man also learned to budget everything from powder and bullets, to salt and sugar. Most of what he ate he could expect the hunters to find and kill as the brigade moved across the mountains. He knew how to preserve meat for the winter by smoking and salting, and learned enough about root vegetables at

Below: *Men seeking the biggest furs – bear – built large dead-fall traps like this one in Colorado, suspending heavy logs over a baited "trigger." When the bear took the bait, the logs fell on the animal, either trapping or killing it.*

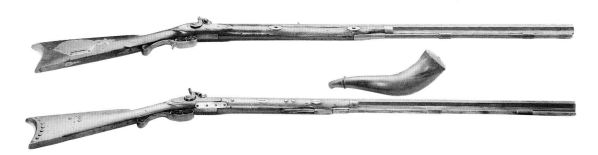

Top: *The famous Hawken Rifle, with its heavy barrel for long range shooting, and its double set triggers that allowed for the lightest touch to fire the percussion gun, gave the hunter a great advantage in the competition for game.*

Above: *Another Hawken Rifle, this one decorated by its owner with the brass tacks so loved by Indians and whites alike as ornamentation. The powder horn was made from a cow horn hollowed out and plugged with turned or carved wooden stoppers.*

least to know what he could find along his path. He knew, too, how much he could expect his horses and mules to carry, for on every trapping foray the load grew steadily greater from the growing weight of the pelts. The wise trapper took no liquor with him to rob him of his wits when he needed them most, but he had a small store of – ineffective – medicine, coffee, sugar or molasses, and perhaps hard bread or flour.

He took particular care of three things – his animals, his traps, and his rifle. If he lost or broke his traps he compromised his whole season, for no other trapper could afford to loan or sell his own. He looked out for the health of his animals, for they brought him into the wilderness and he needed them to get him out again, with or without the peltries he sought. In the worst extremity, they, too, could become food if an early blizzard trapped him in the mountains. And if he lost or broke his gun, or squandered his powder and ball or let it spoil from damp, then he was defenseless in a very inhospitable land, and dependent on others for his protection.

Many men carried their own firearms, preferably a rifled shoulder gun of the Pennsylvania or Kentucky rifle variety. The men outfitted by the companies more often carried cruder, less effective, smoothbore muskets, still frightening and at close range deadly to foemen and game. Until the 1830s virtually all would have been of the flintlock variety, but thereafter the new cap and ball percussion system, with its added speed and dependability, began to be seen in the West.

No trapper or hunter would be without his skinning knife, a universal tool useful for everything from cutting brush and skinning beaver, to digging a fire pit. In an extremity it was even a surgical tool, as was the case with Tom Smith, who in the fall of 1827 was shot in the leg during an Indian fight, the bullet breaking both bones above his left ankle. The only treatment appeared to be amputation, but none of his companions would do it, so he took a butcher's knife and cut through the flesh and tendons himself, hacked through the remaining bits of bone, and then refused to cauterize the wound by thrusting it into a fire. Amazingly, he survived to tell the story.[7]

In the end, those survived who were tough, enduring, and who could learn. The Mountain Man had to know how to trap and shoot, how to ride, climb mountains, and fight with gun , knife, and tomahawk. Working so much in and beside water, he had better be a good swimmer. Moreover, he needed to know – like his Indian neighbors – how to read the wilderness by sight, sound, touch, and even smell. Failure in any one could mean swift death. "Every man carries here emphatically his life in his hand," Ferris himself wrote in the 1830s, "and it is only by the most watchful precaution, grounded upon and guided by the observation of every unnatural appearance however slight, that he can hope to preserve it."[8]

Left: *In the bitterly cold snows of the mountains, the wise trapper took care against frost bite by making extremely warm gloves, like these fashioned from bearskin. They still left enough room for mobility to handle his side knife for skinning or self defense.*

Below left: *Shooting the bear or buffalo, or trapping the beaver, was the easy part. The hard labor came in the skinning and preparing the pelt for preservation and transportation to market. This specially curved iron knife was designed for scraping the inside of a hide clean of flesh and fat.*

CHAPTER FIVE

Overland Emigrant Trains

"A race of perpetual emigrants who roam as dreary waifs over the west."
(A visitor about the Newty family of hog-farmers from
Oregon and California and Montana.)

Below: *Albert Bierstadt's evocative 1867 painting "Emigrants Crossing the Plains" offered a deceptively tranquil portrait of the move west. More likely it was hot, dusty, overcast, with rain and no shade, and everyone afoot.*

A SURPRISING, AND AS yet not fully explained, phenomenon took place about 1840, just as the era of the Mountain Men was coming to an end. Even though there was abundant cheap land available throughout the prairies and plains of latter-day Kansas, Nebraska, Iowa, and more, thousands of Easterners took a sudden passion to carve new homes for themselves on the Pacific coast, first in the Oregon territory, and soon thereafter, with the discovery of

gold, in California. Few could afford the costly passage by ship, especially with families and their worldly possessions. The only alternative was a trek across the continent, some 2,000 miles from St. Louis or Independence and St. Joseph, Missouri, through a wilderness still untamed and only imperfectly understood. And whereas the trappers, at least, knew the native peoples and had learned from them and from experience the ways of survival in such a world, these men and women and children from Ohio and New York, and even from abroad, had no knowledge or experience whatever to prepare them. For the first time in the continent's history to date, a small army of amateurs was about to attempt what even the most seasoned Mountain Men had not done until Jedediah Smith and his ilk.

To prepare them for their challenge to survival, they came armed mainly with rifles, muskets, and shotguns, and the strength of numbers and some organization. Many had guidebooks to warn them of dangers ahead, but far too many such were lurid compendia of rumors written by men with no practical experience. Published maps were few, mainly based on Long's survey, and too general to be of great use in the day-to-day challenge of finding water and wood, crossing a swollen stream, or negotiating a mountain pass.

Thus it was fortuitous that with the fur trade in decline, there was

Above: The people who made the overland trek often came in response to advertisements like this broadside, whose images of railroads and steamboats suggested an easy passage. For some, it was easy indeed; for others a nightmare.

Ho for Kansas!

Brethren, Friends, & Fellow Citizens:
I feel thankful to inform you that the
REAL ESTATE
AND
Homestead Association,
Will Leave Here the
15th of April, 1878,

In pursuit of Homes in the Southwestern
Lands of America, at Transportation
Rates, cheaper than ever
was known before.
For full information inquire of
Benj. Singleton, better known as old Pap,
NO. 5 NORTH FRONT STREET.
Beware of Speculators and Adventurers, as it is a dangerous thing
to fall in their hands.
Nashville, Tenn., March 18, 1878.

Above: *The promise of free or cheap land brought more people west than any other single lure. Entrepreneurs often enticed people with no idea of the challenges and hardships they would face. Many could not stand the life and returned east.*

a small cadre of extremely experienced men – the Mountain Men – looking for employment just at the time that the overland emigration tide began to swell. Sublette, Bridger, and several others became trail guides, capitalizing not only on their knowledge of geography, but also on what they had learned of survival from Indians and their own explorations. From beginning to end on this frontier, the greatest survival skill of all, next to endurance, was knowledge, and what the emigrants did not possess, they could hire, and most did.

Preparedness was next most important, and there the emigrants' performance ranged from the prudent to the pitiful. Most left "civilization" from outfitting towns like Independence and St. Joseph, where they exchanged their cash for the wagons and animals and provisions and tools they would need. This also, in its way, gave them an edge. Certain as it is that many a shady merchant simply cleaned out a "greenhorn," trading on his ignorance to fleece him of his coin, still most of the merchants acquired through their own experience a substantial knowledge of what the emigrant must have as a necessity, and what he could do without, and thus guided his customers toward the best use of their money and the most practical outfit to take with them. The greatest complaint of all among emigrants was hunger from want of taking sufficient food with them, and when two trains met,

there were inevitably those members trying desperately to get others to part with some of their stores. Moreover, in these towns the neophyte from the East could learn how to hitch his oxen to his new wagon and how to drive both, how to pack his horses and mules, how to cook on the trail, and how to load and fire a rifle.[1]

Once on the trail, sheer numbers gave them some protection. In 1848, before the Gold Rush exaggerated everything tenfold, more than 4,000 people made the trek west along the Oregon and California trails. It was nothing for a rider to pass 200 or even 300 wagons on the trail in a single day.[2] Emigrants formed themselves into companies, sometimes sponsored by syndicates and subscription firms in the East. This guaranteed them enough manpower to push wagons up steep hills, control animals in stream crossings, and defend themselves against attack. The lone emigrant wagon stood

Above: *It could look beautiful, and was, but to the untested new settler landscapes like this in the Wind River Mountains in Wyoming presented terrifying prospects. How were they to survive the winters, build homes, or withstand the isolation?*

Above: *Perhaps the least prepared of all for the rigors of frontier survival were the dreamy-eyed, get-rich-quick men with visions of gold and silver. For every Forty-Niner who went to California looking for a big strike, thousands came and failed, and not a few perished.*

greatly reduced chances of making it to Oregon, being easy prey to everything from a broken wagon wheel to opportunistic natives, or even wolves. Moreover, by pooling their resources, the stronger could assist the weaker, the provident could help bail out the improvident, and from among their merged funds they could afford to hire the sort of guides and assistance that gave them a greatly enhanced chance of success. Many trains also hired doctors if they did not already have physicians among their number. With the cholera and other health

Below: *Not just white Europeans came to face the hazards and reap the riches. Men like these Chinese went to the gold camps, either to prospect for themselves, or to work for others, and some faced resentment and racism.*

Above: *A typical wagon "train" looked more like this image of two or three families stopping along the road on the way to California in the 1860s. Not surprisingly, every man in the photo holds a rifle, for out here survival depended on preparedness at all times.*

Opposite: *Definitely not the heavy-duty Conestoga type of wagon, this lightweight affair would not likely survive the trek from Independence to Oregon. This is probably a family making a short move.*

hazards ahead, the company without some medical expertise faced much increased hazard. At the same time, for all the inevitable friction that close association for months would produce, they would also be laying within themselves the seeds of future community and social relations, just as necessary for survival if and when they reached their promised land.

As with the early explorers, so also the emigrants gradually built a store of knowledge, each successive company learning from its predecessors thanks to an ingenious "roadside telegraph," as it was called. If a wagon train learned something valuable about water or grass, a river crossing or Indian threat, members simply wrote messages on paper or cloth and left them tied to sticks or saplings beside the trail, to be found by those coming after, most of whom read them and then left them undisturbed for yet other future readers. Sometimes the emigrants carved their messages into trees or onto boulders, and even left information on animal skulls, leading some to talk about the "Bone Express."[3] Whatever it was called, it could make the difference between life and disaster, with warnings of road forks and hazards, poisoned water, or worse.

Right: *Making camp on the Front Range of the Rockies, these men, probably a hunting or surveying party, are none too tidy in their campsite, and clearly show the lack of attention to safety that suggests there is no danger of Indian marauders in the vicinity.*

Surprisingly enough, and contrary to popular myth, part of the reason that overland emigrants managed to survive was the active cooperation and assistance of the native peoples through whose lands they passed. In Oregon in 1846 one observer looked on as "emigrants and Indians meet, it appears, for the purpose of affording mutual aid."[4] In spite of the fact that Indians represented really the only substantial threat of violent death to overland pioneers, killing hundreds during the two decades that the overland trails flourished, in reality they provided far more in the way of co-operation.

For a start, in the earliest days of the wagon migration westward, it was from the natives that most emigrants got information on the best routes, the location of water, firewood, grass for grazing, where game could be found, the bogs to avoid, and even the other native tribes to watch out for. Often Indians themselves served as trail guides for emigrant parties. One of the most heavily traveled routes into California, the Truckee River trail, was named by whites for the Paiute leader who revealed it to them.

MAP AS AT 1840 TERRITORY

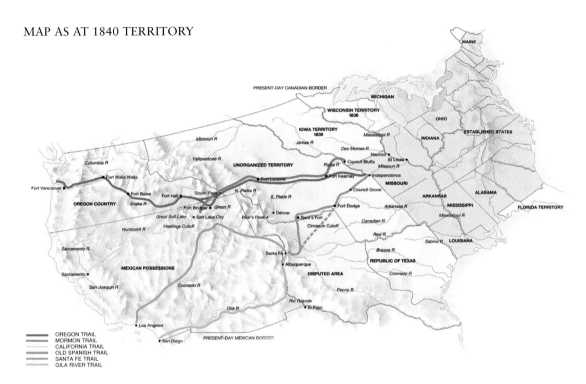

Trail legend:
- OREGON TRAIL
- MORMON TRAIL
- CALIFORNIA TRAIL
- OLD SPANISH TRAIL
- SANTA FE TRAIL
- GILA RIVER TRAIL

Above: *In their quest west, the pioneers utilized a number of emigrant trails, some following the Lewis and Clark exploration route, others using the old trading routes like the Santa Fe Trail. The northern routes like the Oregon Trail and the Mormon Trail depended on South Pass to get them through the Rockies, and then the Oregon Trail followed the line of the Snake River to the Columbia, meaning that fresh water was almost always available and the bottomland along the rivers usually allowed a smooth road, though there were falls and other obstacles that sometimes required exhausting and hazardous portages. The California Trail branched off from the Oregon route, and followed the Humboldt River into Nevada before it crossed the desert to the Sierras. It could be extremely hazardous in the wrong weather, as the ill-fated Donner party discovered. To the south, emigrants took the Santa Fe Trail to its terminus, and there picked up the new Gila River route across Arizona to the Colorado River before entering California. Even then the last run to San Diego could be dangerous across unforgiving desert wastes. To the north ran the Old Spanish Trail, something of a misnomer since it was not used by the Spaniards.*

To be sure, sometimes the information was coerced by parties who kidnapped Indians and forced them to act as guides before their release, and however less than admirable such a course might be, still it proved an effective way of overcoming an obstacle to safety and survival. Most often the guides went voluntarily, however, and some tribes like the Paiutes and Shoshones became known for their willingness to be of assistance. Part of the motivation, of course, might have been that by guiding the whites through their land and on to the West, the Indians hoped that the intruders would not settle and compete with them for their own hunting grounds.

Beyond this, natives worked on many trains as drovers, teamsters,

Below: A typical "prairie schooner," this adaptation of the earlier Conestoga wagon was designed for heavy travel over rough terrain, from its iron-shod wheels and iron axles, to its simple but efficient shape. It could carry much, withstand a lot, and become a boat, or even a sled if it had to.

or helped get wagons and stock across difficult river crossings. Trains headed for Oregon used such Indian help extensively, the simple logic being that since they did not know the intricacies of the landscape themselves, and had no intention of staying long enough to learn, the only option was to hire the only local experts available. Emigrants paid with the usual trade trinkets, and the prudent invested in a considerable stock, expecting that the return for the modest investment could well be life or death. More than one emigrant later complained, in fact, that he could not find enough Indians along the trail to trade with for services. Some native guides chose their own payment by simply riding off on a selected animal without asking permission.

The alternative, if no experienced white guides were available, was to risk crossings and trails on their own, and many an inexperienced train met disaster. Drownings in rapids were common without the aid of Indian rowers. Moreover, the natives acted as guards and night watchmen over stock and wagons in uncertain territory, and in some instances, actually lent the weight of their bows against rival tribes when emigrants were attacked. Along the way they showed the whites what roots and plants were safe to eat to supplement their often monotonous – and scarce – diet.

Simply being prepared to trade with the natives for clothing, hides, even tools and weapons, helped the emigrants' chances of successfully completing their journeys, while the stocks of food they could buy from them – everything from smoked salmon to corn to pumpkins – saved many lives, especially from the threat of scurvy as vegetables brought with them from home quickly ran out or spoiled. In return, the whites gave clothing, arms and ammunition, food, tobacco, soap, fish hooks, medicine, and in one case umbrellas![5] Alcohol sometimes became currency, too, though the wiser emigrants soon learned that giving too much whisky to peoples unused to it too often led to mayhem and brawls. Some tribes, notably the Sioux and Pawnee, also demanded tribute, virtually a "toll," for passing safely through their lands, and for the guarantee of going unmolested most emigrants were happy to offer up something in compensation. Moreover, with rare exceptions, the Indians were as good as their word once the toll was paid.[6]

Above: *A typical pioneer family and their gear on the trail. This couple and their six children appear to be well outfitted, though the average family traveling west would be with a group of families for mutual protection.*

Attack by the natives

Inevitably, nevertheless, there would be conflicts and outbreaks of violence despite the best efforts at diplomacy on both sides. "We are continually hearing of the depredations of the Indians but we have not seen one yet," wrote an emigrant woman in 1851.[7] Indeed, most stories of attacks on wagon trains were mere rumor and exaggeration, but whites who started out on the trails from Missouri came armed nevertheless with a store of received wisdom on how to comport themselves. They must not let the natives see fear, was the prime dictum. Sensing that gave the Indians the upper hand, so it was thought. Instead, and to counter any real trepidation, guidebooks admonished emigrants to show constant vigilance by day and night. They should keep themselves apart from any nearby bands of natives and not let them intermingle for fear of a surprise attack. They should not yield to excessive native demands for food or tribute, for that, too, would be a sign of fear and fear meant vulnerability. They must always be ready with threats of their own, from whipping to shooting, to keep unruly Indians from getting out of hand. As a result, despite the friendly relations encountered by most, still almost all emigrants regarded the natives with a substantial degree of distrust, and, however unfair it may have been, the consequent caution undoubtedly worked to their benefit on those occasions when they encountered genuine hostility.[8]

Actual massacres of whole wagon parties were few. Almost always such attacks were against small trains of half a dozen wagons or fewer, and then only when they were on the trail during the day and

Below: The most familiar sight on the emigrant trails would be the endless line of wagons like this one, with its horses and oxen and cattle, the men and women walking beside the wagons, the children walking or inside. In numbers like this, and with the wagons themselves for defense, these settlers were fairly safe from Indian attack.

Right: *Powder Face, an Arapaho chief shown circa 1870, carries the crooked lance of the Spear Society showing that he is a warrior to die before retreating in battle. A face to face encounter with him was not likely to turn out happily for a settler if the Arapaho were on the war path. Indians presented a greater threat to pioneer livestock than to the people themselves, but enough unprepared or unlucky settlers died all the same.*

spread out rather than circled or corralled for defense. As long as they kept their heads, even a relatively small group of emigrants had little to fear so long as they stayed together, remained vigilant, and kept risks to a minimum. Sometimes the greater risk in an Indian attack came from emigrants running and abandoning animals and wagons in their fright. Even if they escaped pursuit, now they faced reduced mobility and starvation, and if they lost their guides they could wander for weeks before being found, if ever.

More than one such group had to resort to cannibalism to stay alive as some of their group succumbed, and of course the saga of the Donner party in 1846, when cut off by snow in the Sierras, became symbolic of the extremities to which hunger could force unlucky or improvident emigrants. Yet even they, in their macabre way, demonstrated the ultimate lengths to which these westering people would go in order to survive. Eating each other may not exactly have been a "skill," but it was a means to stay alive.

Below: *This wagon train camped near Boulder, Colorado, has eschewed the traditional circling of the wagons for protection since it is in a peaceful region. Interestingly, the canvas covers are white in spite of the dirt of the trail. That was the sun bleaching them, and showed how necessary they were to protect children and the elderly from exposure.*

CHAPTER SIX

Hunters and Settlers

"We kill buffaloes for food and clothing. Your young men shoot for pleasure."
(Sitting Bull of the Hunkpapa Sioux)

Opposite: *Those who lived on the Plains and in the mountains needed to acquire an arsenal of skills, many of which were the same regardless of whether they were native or white. These Cheyenne have staked out buffalo hides and are scraping them prior to tanning. Settlers would do exactly the same thing.*

ONCE THEY PUT down their roots, the men and women who settled the new frontier only lay aside the hazards of the journey to their new lives to take up a different challenge requiring yet another set of skills in order to survive. Establishing shelter and livelihood could be just as chancy as encountering hostile natives and uncharted wastes when it came to eking a living out of what was still, in many ways, a wilderness. This was especially so for the kind of people who came from a life east of the Mississippi that might as well have been that of a different planet for all it prepared them for the frontier.

For a few, the change was not so great, as they simply exchanged one migratory exploitative occupation for another. The Mountain Men and the trail drivers and guides who lived long enough and chose not to settle down could merely turn to a different outdoor way of life, and the most obvious was the commercial hunting of the bison. Upwards of sixty million American bison – more commonly called buffalo – inhabited the prairies and Great Plains as the era of the Mountain Man gave way to the day of the farmer and stockman.

To the native peoples, of course, the animal represented food, clothing, shelter, even religion. To the early whites in the region, on the other hand, the teeming seas of the beasts were food to be sure, but largely a nuisance. The land could not be put under the plow or checkered with fences until the massive herds no longer roamed

rough over the landscape. Large scale hunting was the only solution to that problem.

Professional buffalo hunters

While some few whites began to support themselves by buffalo hunting, the profession really did not get into full swing until after the Civil War of 1861-65. The large caliber .58 rifles left over from the war were powerful enough to bring down an animal. Even more powerful were the breechloading weapons that followed, especially the Sharps rifle in its various calibers, the most popular being .45 with a massive powder charge.

Below: *A buffalo hunter armed with a Sharps Rifle has brought down half a dozen bison, and is about the skin them in the snow. It was a means of living until the bison were all but hunted out of existence.*

Left: *A typical bison hunter carried a high-powered, large bore rifle, like this .45 Sharps sporting rifle. From a good stand, with plenty of ammunition, he could bring down twenty or more at a time before a herd actually smelled him and moved on. Survival, here, was a challenge for the bison and not man.*

Above: *A party of buffalo hunters near Sheridan, Kansas, have set up quarters for a long hunt, with a dugout house, racks for drying joints of meat, and for these two men a little time to clean their Sharps rifles. Few men stayed in the trade for very long.*

Like all before him, the white buffalo hunter needed an understanding of basic survival skills to stay alive on the open prairie. He had to know the territory. He needed to pack sufficient provisions for the long hunt and have enough pack animals, and kept in top condition, for them to haul out the object of the hunt, the bison furs. He had to be provident with his supplies and wary of his surroundings if he hunted close to native peoples not on friendly terms with whites.

As the latter half of the nineteenth century wore on, and the Indians became more and more confined, this became less a concern. Still, the white hunter had to be able to sleep out on the prairies, often for months on the hunt. Most buffalo hunters resorted to dugout pits covered with boughs for evening shelter, or made small huts of sod in miniature models of the larger "soddies" built by settlers. Besides his big bore rifle, he equipped himself with a cartridge belt or else large pockets on his hunting coat or shirt, to make certain that he had ample ammunition at hand when he took his stand. He needed skinning knives, a heavy coat often made of bison fur itself for warmth on cold prairie nights, perhaps a pistol for more wieldy personal protection.

The hunter's skills

However, the buffalo hunter had to learn new skills not required of the subsistence hunters of the plains in earlier generations. For him now efficiency was a question of time, energy, and equipment. First, he needed to know where to find the bison. In the early days this was no problem, since they were practically everywhere in two vast herds. The northern herd ranged across latter-day Montana, the Dakotas, and upper Wyoming, while the southern herd covered southern Wyoming, Kansas, Nebraska, Oklahoma, and part of Texas. Once a hunter got himself to the right territory and at the right season, the animals almost came to him. In later years, however, as hunting thinned the herds and the restriction of their ranges increased thanks to the fence and the plow, the hunter had to know more and more about bison habits in order to find them. He also had to learn about the bison's grazing, the poor senses of hearing and smell that could allow a hunter to approach close enough for a shot undetected, and the placid disposition of the animals so long as not unduly spooked.

The beast's poor hearing was especially useful to the canny hunter. If he shot one animal then went in to collect the hide, he could expect to scare away the rest of those grazing in the vicinity. That meant that after he skinned the one beast, he had to pack the pelt, mount, and find the herd again, stalk to a likely spot, and repeat the process, a considerable squandering of what might otherwise have been productive and profitable hunting time. However, before long the better hunters learned that with a rifle powerful enough to deliver a slug with killing force at more than 200 yards, they could fire from a

Below: *The essential articles of support and survival for the buffalo hunter. Foremost were his weapons. The .45-60 Winchester 1873 lever-action repeating rifle at left was ideal for bringing down the big game, as was the .50 caliber Spencer repeating rifle at right. The Sharps Rifle, this one the 1874 .45 sport model, was a perennial mainstay of the trade, and regardless of the rifle used the hunter had to have a cartridge belt to keep the bullets secure and reliably handy. The skinning knife on the coat performed a variety of functions besides removing hides from the carcasses. The heavy winter coat, itself made of bison hide, kept a man warm on a long vigil at the stand, while the rolled piece of tanned buffalo hide or the buffalo calf hide underneath it could be put to any number of uses. In a close quarters situation, the .45 Colt Single Action Army revolver, or "Peacemaker," at right, could save his life if he encountered a deadly snake or two-legged threat. Not every buffalo hunter would have each of these articles, but all would be familiar, and most were to be found in any hunter's baggage. The rawhide-covered bone pack saddle at top center provided the anchor to get all of his "trappings" aboard the hunter's mules and horses.*

Left: *In the buffalo trade, it was the bison whose survival was threatened. More than 1.5 million of them were killed just in a two-year period in the 1870s. What was left after the hides were taken were the bones, mountains of them, and in 1874 alone 3,500 tons of bones were sold east to make fertilizer.*

distance great enough that the sound of the rifle firing did not startle the herd. If he selected a good stand, then, the hunter could pick off one animal after another, and all the remaining bison knew was that every few minutes one of their number just slumped to the ground. Until the beasts smelled blood and recognized the scent of danger, a hunter might bring down a score or more, and then when finally the herd moved on, he could come in with his skinning knife and efficiently spend the rest of the day – even several days – harvesting hides. Some hunters were successful on an industrial scale, specializing just in the killing, while hired "skinners" followed behind to remove the hides from the carcasses.[1]

Efficiency such as this ravaged the herds. One hunter could reasonably hope to take 1,000 hides a year, and there were hundreds of hunters out for the $2 to $3 each they could get for a pelt. The animals' bones, too, had value as fertilizer. In just the two years 1872-74 one railroad in Kansas hauled out more than one and one-half million hides. Multiply that by the other many hunting grounds and there's little surprise that within a generation the herds were almost hunted out of existence. The southern herd was all but gone by 1878; the northern herd was reduced to near extinction by the late 1880s. And as an added benefit for the survival of white settlers, the disappearance of the bison also dramatically limited the range and health of the Plains Indians whose existence had for so long been so intimately tied with that of the buffalo.[2]

Settlers' crafts

For those who chose the soil for their livelihood, there were other skills needed, other attributes essential. For a start, one virtual necessity was manpower, meaning males. Whether it be erecting a house, wielding axe and saw to cut down trees to clear a field, harnessing a team of horses or oxen to pull the stumps from the cleared acreage, or planting and then harvesting the crops to follow, men were essential, and they must be muscular, healthy, and well fed.

Below: Different settlers needed different skills, even in peaceful times. This group of Latter Day Saint, or Mormon, elders, wives, and children, found that for them survival meant getting away from proximity to other more conventional religious denominations. They settled in the wilds of Utah.

Above: *Farmers and homesteaders required a host of specialized tools for all of the tasks they had to perform. At left is a box of general tools, files, a plane, an iron-bound maul, and a number of chisels. A bow saw rests against the box, and beneath it are a broadaxe, an adze, and a froe for splitting shingles, as well as hand shears for shearing sheep. Above them a stump acts as a chopping block, with a double-headed axe embedded in it. The small barrel could be used for anything, but originally probably held some sort of dry goods. The farmer could be sure to reuse it again and again for his own purposes. In front of the block an iron-bladed plow is ready to break the Plains, and resting in its shaft at right is the harness necessary to set a horse or mule to pull the plow. Across the bottom of the picture sits a scythe for reaping grain and cutting grass, and above it at center are wooden eating utensils, a two-tined pitchfork head, a cast iron Dutch oven, a ceramic jug, a round wooden pestle for mashing potatoes and turnips, and a carved wooden bowl with a wooden fork on top.*

Above: *A not untypical ranch in the new settlements might look like this, rude buildings, all manner of livestock, a couple of log cabins and pens, and a lot of children. All were needed, even the children, to get done the work of planting, harvesting, shearing, butchering, and every other task that kept the whole family surviving.*

They might also have to know the skills – and have the strength – to do blacksmithing, tanning hides, making furniture, cobbling crude shoes, or any other task that came to hand. And all of that required, besides strength and dexterity, an ability to learn quickly. Few needed to become accomplished masters at any such craft, but all needed to know the rudiments in order to mend the broken plow, put an edge on a dull blade, prepare a hide for its leather to make a saddle, and so much more.

To be sure, women were essential as well, to tend the kitchen gardens, cook, raise the children, help with the harvest and preserve the vegetables. Careful division of labor based on skills and ability was a necessity, and many women even helped with the plowing. But in the end, while a male settler by himself or with one or two others could make a go of a homestead on the plains, a woman on her own stood very little chance of survival. It was a land that required strength and brute force to match its own. Nevertheless, even among the men, those most likely to succeed were those with families. The family made a small social unit to preserve sanity on the isolated frontier. The sons helped with the heavy work, the daughters with the home chores, yet each bolstered the spirit and resolve of the other.[3]

Most brought with them the knowledge of agriculture and livestock care that was to support them materially. Raising corn was much the same whether in Ohio or Kansas, and tending pigs and cows differed little either, except in the larger acreage most settlers acquired. That allowed them to let their animals depend rather more on grazing than on fodder furnished by humans, but on the other hand it imposed on the settlers an added onus of extensive fence building and tending, especially against the threat of the occasional marauding Indian or a stampeding bison herd.

Settlers' houses

The real challenge was their house. Settlers came almost exclusively from areas of the Union – or the world – where wood or stone or the ingredients for brick had been abundant, and a man could find the materials for making his own home on his own soil. Out on the prairies and plains, however, trees could be scarce, and those that existed often proved too gnarly and bent to make timber. Stone was scarce, and so was brick clay. The only remaining resort, especially for that first house so necessary to get a farm going, was the ground itself. With time and, they hoped, prosperity, settlers could afford to buy lumber and nails and make a proper house.

Until then, they dug the topsoil sod in large clumps perhaps up to six inches thick and a foot wide by eighteen inches long. They let it dry out through the summer and then used it as building blocks like brick, usually making rudimentary one-room houses at first, but in time learning to produce rather extensive multi-room dwellings. As the grass in the sod continued to grow in summer and fall, the roots spread to keep the earth from breaking up and to form walls into a

Above: *When settlers first arrived on their new claims, especially on the Plains, they often built these sod dugouts, with only sash windows and a wooden door to remind them of more conventional construction. Some would live in their "soddies" for years, more like cave dwellers than what they had been in the East.*

single mass, aided by rains.[4] Moreover, when the grass grew on the exterior of the walls, it repelled the rain and damp.

That did not mean that the interior was either dry or very comfortable. There was no keeping a "soddy" clean, even when affluence allowed the laying of a board floor to replace the bare ground. The roof had to be of timbers, often itself covered with sod, and that meant a constant dribble of dust into the interior. Insects thrived in the walls, worms bored through them, and vermin from outside, including poisonous snakes, sought the cool interiors. But this was a house that would not burn down even in a prairie fire, and in the heat of the summer its walls kept the inside relatively cool and habitable.[5]

Besides being the builder of his house – of whatever material – the settler had to know how to locate likely spots to find water and then dig and line a well, or else take the risk of flood by settling his family near or beside a stream of running water that could be depended upon to flow all year. Even then, he collected rainwater when he could, especially since typhoid could make water holes and springs contaminated.

Settlers had to learn how to find firewood where there were no forests, in order to cook and provide heat for their homes in winter, especially on the plains where blizzards could bury a house in drifts. The bison helped there, for the settlers quickly adopted the Indian practice of using dried buffalo dung – dirty and smelly as it was – to burn. Prairie grass, and even dried sod could be burned as well.

And for all of them, spiritual survival was essential to combat the

Left: *Surviving could be hard on the sensibilities as well as the back. Frontier women who went west to the Plains likely never imagined that to keep their homes warm in a treeless expanse they would collect dried buffalo dung to burn in the fireplaces and stoves. Her grimace may be as much distaste as strain at the weight.*

Above: *Smart settlers depended on the ever-present pig, which had been a mainstay of rural farm life, especially in the South. The swine could thrive on almost anything, could fend for themselves, eat the stubble left from a corn harvest, and became hams and bacon and sausage and scrapple and lard.*

isolation, the loneliness, and the multiple discouragements that nature hurled at them. Sometimes even before building their homes, they set aside a grove for a church or a school. They made holidays communal affairs, and soon made house building and barn raising a community effort as well, binding the settler families to each other in mutual dependency and mutual indebtedness. For the same reasons, marriage was an essential institution, and even poor matches lasted out of mutual dependency. For settlers, as for all those who confronted the frontier before them, endurance and survival were most important of all, and only their means toward those ends set them apart from all who challenged the wilderness.[6]

Left: *A husband and sturdy wife work the soil outside their elaborate sod house. Plowing was back-breaking work even with a horse to pull the plow, yet women and even children would learn to rein the draft animals and break the soil.*

Below: *Church provided the main source of community for settlers, as for this group of worshippers near Bluff City, Iowa, outside their sod chapel. Such social gatherings were essential for mental as well as spiritual health.*

CHAPTER SEVEN

The Frontier Army

"You were part of a proud outfit that had a fighting reputation,
and you were ready for a fight or a frolic."
(Private Charles Windolph recalling his days with the Seventh Cavalry)

USEFUL AS IT WAS for individuals and small informal groups of trappers or settlers to draw much – if not most – of their survival adaptation to the West from the native inhabitants, it was neither always possible nor advisable for larger, more organized groups to follow suit. Culture, profession, and logic dictated that when the United States Army crossed the Mississippi after the Louisiana Purchase and began to fulfill its role of exploring and mapping the

Right: *The Frontier Army had the task of protecting settlers and travelers as they encountered the new West. Both infantry and cavalry took on the task, including these "Buffalo Soldiers," black men enlisted to make careers in the military.*

frontier, and keeping the peace, it would have to answer to other imperatives. An institution that by its nature was founded on discipline, the application where necessary of substantial force, and obedience to civilian rulers in Washington, simply could not encourage or allow its men to be as individualist as the Mountain Men. That meant that survival and coping skills that suited a man or a few men alone might not work for a company or a regiment of soldiers, with their specialized needs, objectives, equipment, and animals. Moreover, individualism was simply foreign to the military mind throughout the world.

It began with simple transportation. Soldiers came to the West by many means, by horse and by square-rigger in the early days, by steamboat and railroad in later decades, and also by foot throughout. The vital nature of the foot gear of a soldier was evidenced by the fact that, in the 1840s for instance, standard allowance to a soldier for a five-year enlistment included more pairs of stockings and boots than any other article of apparel. One overcoat was expected to last him his entire term, and each of three dress coats was expected not to wear out for twenty months. His trousers were given six months to a pair before they were replaced, while every pair of "drawers" or

Left: Napoleon may have said that an army marched on its stomach, but any foot soldier in the West knew that the most essential article of clothing in his kit was his pair of boots. Without them he was all but immobile, unable either to protect civilians or even to do much for himself.

Above: Some soldiers wore shoes or brogans, though boots were preferred because they protected shins and calves against brush scratches. Moreover, in an extremity, the boot top could be cut off and used for an ersatz sole repair.

underwear had a life expectancy of seven-and-one-half months. But the government, knowing that a soldier's life was marching over rough roads or no roads at all, allowed him twenty pairs of socks and boots, expecting each to last just three months before becoming worn out. Even this was inadequate, however, for it was calculated for the experience of a soldier in the East on garrison duty. "Poor old shoes!" a soldier lamented in the 1840s when they wore out. "I lay you off with many regrets – not that you have untruly failed, but that I may get another pair broke for Service." The man who lost his shoes on the march could face hard rocks, burning sand, even cactus spikes and the like, and throughout the army's frontier experience, sore feet would take more men out of line than Indian arrows.[1]

It soon became apparent that Western soldiers walked through their boot soles – and everything else – much faster, while at the same time being much farther from sources of resupply. Exposure, wear, loss on the march, and the usual lack of care by the inattentive,

Right: *A cavalryman's equipment on the frontier varied widely and changed periodically. The 1842 H. Aston .54 caliber horse pistol at bottom was widely used before the Civil War, but after 1860 the horsemen carried the Colt Model 1860 .44 revolver, its cartridges coming in the paper packages shown here. The yellow-faced shell jacket was standard issue for a cavalryman.*

required more, and placed a heavy responsibility on the soldier to take every care possible with what he had while he had it, for a new issue of clothing and equipment could be months away. The army offered cash incentives to soldiers who managed to care for and preserve articles of their uniform. Meanwhile, acknowledging the havoc that heat stroke could play with improperly dressed men on the march, it also allowed them cotton shirts and uniforms for service in the warm months of May through September, and wool and flannel outfits for the colder months, to promote some degree of comfort. Indeed, some officers regularly allowed exceptions to uniform dress rules when on campaign in respect of exigencies of

Above: *The Model 1861 .58 caliber rifled musket was a standard weapon of the frontier infantry until after the Civil War. It fired the paper cartridges shown below it, the bullet and power load encased in a paper tube, while above it are percussion caps, which the hammer actually hit to ignite the powder.*

Left: *The artillery was a common sight in the West, too, though perhaps it played a less ubiquitous role in defense than infantry and cavalry. The shell jacket carries the red facings of the branch of service. The hat, or kepi in the French style, shows the bugle insignia of the infantry.*

91

weather and terrain, and the breakdown of supply lines that should have brought replacement articles. Shortly after the end of the war with Mexico in 1848, Congress abolished the allowance per soldier, and instead just authorized issuing replacements on an as-needed basis.[2] The prudent soldier learned to carry needle and thread as part of his basic tackle in the meantime.

Looking after the equipment

The soldier's equipment was just as important. He got a canteen, and if he did not care for it, but instead allowed it to rust or suffer a puncture, or if he lost it, he imperiled his life. Similarly, he was issued a rubber-coated haversack in which to keep dry his rations and other personal effects, including extra clothing. Loss of or damage to that could mean that such vital materials could mildew and rot. If he was to have hot meals when opportunity afforded, he had to care for the cooking tools used by his mess, and also the harness for pack and wagon animals that hauled his tents and heavier equipment.

If transportation broke down on campaign in the wilderness, then the soldiers faced the painful option of trying to carry everything on their own backs, meaning greater discomfort and risk of exhaustion, or else abandoning what they could not carry despite the possibility of needing it later. Soldiers also needed to know to

Right: *Next to his boots, the soldier's most essential kit on the march was his canteen, especially in the arid Plains. This Model 1858 tin canteen is in a cotton sling and covering, which had the benefit of absorbing water if soaked in a stream, thus keeping the contents cool for a few hours.*

Far right: *The Model 1855 standard-issue bag pattern knapsack was the soldier's larder, dresser, and trunk. What he needed to survive in the field for several days at a time he carried on his back in his knapsack. In addition to rations and sewing kit, there might be a book, a bible, photos of loved ones, and the like.*

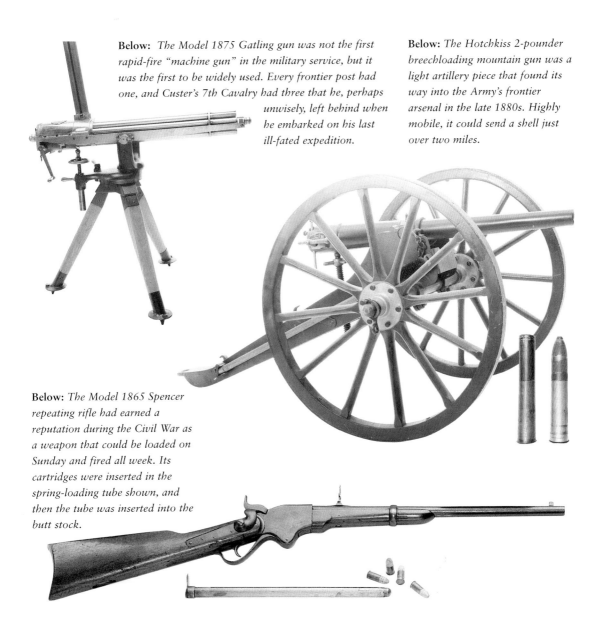

Below: *The Model 1875 Gatling gun was not the first rapid-fire "machine gun" in the military service, but it was the first to be widely used. Every frontier post had one, and Custer's 7th Cavalry had three that he, perhaps unwisely, left behind when he embarked on his last ill-fated expedition.*

Below: *The Hotchkiss 2-pounder breechloading mountain gun was a light artillery piece that found its way into the Army's frontier arsenal in the late 1880s. Highly mobile, it could send a shell just over two miles.*

Below: *The Model 1865 Spencer repeating rifle had earned a reputation during the Civil War as a weapon that could be loaded on Sunday and fired all week. Its cartridges were inserted in the spring-loading tube shown, and then the tube was inserted into the butt stock.*

be careful with their weapons and, besides keeping them in good condition, to treat them respectfully; once it emerged from a gun barrel, a bullet did not discriminate between friend and foe. The frontier army experienced almost as many self-inflicted injuries from accidents and carelessness as it did from hostiles.

Feeding the soldier

No soldier expressed much delight with army rations, which often came in short supply and atrocious condition, and the men quickly learned to forage on their own to supplement their diet. They fished in rivers and streams, caught shellfish on the coast, hunted for game

Below: *A typical frontier fort in the West was designed not so much as a fort in the old stockade sense, but rather as a garrison post, though still one that could be defended. Posts like Fort Marcy at Santa Fe had little fear of being attacked, but could host refugee civilians in time of native uprisings.*

Left: *When it came to survival, the frontier soldiers were not so proud that they could not learn a few things from their Indian adversaries, like this travois being used to haul a wounded man out of the Dakota Badlands during General George Crooks' 1876 campaign against the Sioux.*

when given the opportunity, and sometimes did borrow a page from the Indians' book of experience by harvesting wild vegetables and fruit. They also had to learn to cook their food properly, for undercooked vegetables could cause indigestion, and fruit eaten before it was ripe led to diarrhea. Picking wild plums in the still unexplored territory around the Canadian River north of Texas might have been fun for soldiers with an army expedition in 1845, but when they made the fruit into a plum pudding, the result was upset stomachs and "bad consequences," one lamented.[3]   And when they got sick, contradictory as it seemed, strong survival instincts in some soldiers saved their lives by their refusal to go to or remain in army hospital camps, where overcrowding and medical ignorance prevailed, and deadly microbes flourished. Regarding an ignorant or uncaring army doctor as an enemy was

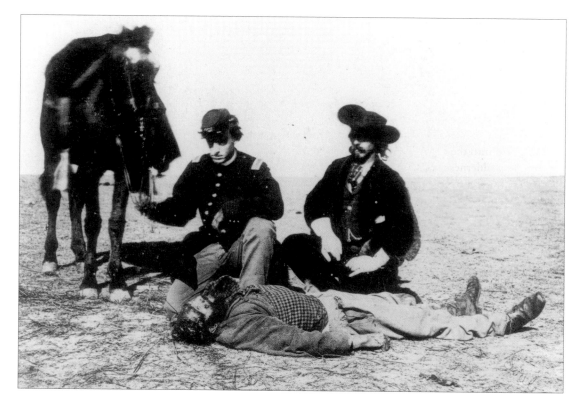

Above: *When hostilities with the natives were under way, the price of carelessness could be terrible. This civilian has paid it with the loss of his life and a part of his scalp. There were few second chances in the wilderness if a man or woman got separated from the means of defense.*

often the first step on the road to recovery.

Foraging and cooking and eating in messes of half a dozen or so also helped develop habits of friendship, trust, and interdependence within the mess that could extend to other areas of vital importance, especially when it came to a fight. Such friendships also helped pass the tedious hours in camp or in garrison, keeping the men's minds active and healthy. "These is my friends," one officer wrote of his messmates, "for they have been tried in places where a man can tell whether men is his friends or not."[4] As a result, for a soldier a real survival skill could be simply knowing how to choose his friends and messmates. One veteran classified soldiers into three categories. The worthless and undependable soldiers he called "dead beats"; the men who were steady and dependable, thrifty and temperate, if unlikely ever to do more than they were told, he regarded as "old soldiers"; and the men who took risks, ran into the fight, played hard, volunteered for anything, and kept themselves ever-ready for action, were called "dare devils." Those last, he said, were "the pride of their officers and the admiration of their companions."[5]

All of such necessities were put under heavy pressure when the soldiers went into the field, whether to campaign against Indians, or explore the wilderness. Bad water was a constant threat. Exposure had to be anticipated. In an era when proper sanitation was little understood, they needed to know enough not to locate their "sinks" or privies upstream of their water supply. Just keeping a camp site relatively neat and clear of things like food scraps could discourage disease-bearing vermin. Keeping themselves and their clothing clean discouraged lice and other potentially deadly parasites, though it usually took vigilant officers to make the men observe such rudiments.

On the march a man had to keep up, for if he straggled behind out of sight of his column, he was an easy mark for a hostile foe, yet another reason to have plenty of water and to dress coolly so as to discourage the sunstroke that accounted for most straggling. "The men seem to have little judgment about leaving the main body," a lieutenant wrote in 1847, "but just go where their inclination leads them." Sometimes it led them to a lonely and violent death.[6]

Organization and discipline

That was where the discipline came into play. Obedience was essential to the military, in peace or war, but especially in the latter. Though their officers might have no more frontier experience than the men, still there were certain procedures for defense that even the neophytes could follow that enhanced chances of safety in a moment of danger. But by and large the officers did have more experience than the men. They knew enough to read the signs of a hostile presence. Vigilance was essential. "A quick eye and a good horse mean life to a man in an Indian country," John C. Frémont recalled of his frontier service. In 1846 Frémont himself, knowing this lesson, neglected to put men on guard around his camp one night, and personally had to go out in the dark, pistol drawn, to scare away Indians whom his animals' behavior suggested were lurking among them. "A mule is a good sentinel," Frémont declared, and that was another survival attribute necessary to the frontier army – how to know from the nervous behavior of the animals in a corral or tethered near camp that a danger was present.[7]

The prudent commander put out guards in sufficient numbers and at a secure enough distance that, even if some were surprised by a foe, still enough would survive to be able to raise the alarm, and with enough time to rouse and prepare the men in the main camp. He also knew where to locate his camp – close enough to water and fuel for the comfort and health of the men, yet behind or atop some natural feature that gave them protection from or the advantage of elevation over any attacker. If especially wary, an officer had his men "sleep on their arms," meaning virtually sleeping with their muskets or rifles by their sides rather than stacking them according to regulation. It bought that extra few seconds that could mean life or death.

Such vigilance remained a standing requisite for survival throughout the frontier period. Against accident and carelessness it was perpetually necessary. Against the Indians, it remained the same until the 1890s when the last

Right: *Shown here during the Civil War, Major General John Charles Frémont, the so-called "Pathfinder," proved to be an inept military commander of armies, but before the war, in the West, he had performed feats of exploration, and developed some of the standard skills for protecting small parties of men in a hostile land.*

hostilities concluded and the native peoples of the continent no longer posed a threat to the soldier's security. The passage of time also lessened – but did not eliminate – the other hazards to be faced. The spread of the railroad made it easier to get replacement clothing and equipment to the men, while modernization of manufacturing made clothing easier and cheaper to produce – economy being ever a concern of the military. Means of preserving food and greater understanding of nutrition meant that soldiers faced fewer hazards from their diet, while better transportation and locally grown foodstuffs in the wake of civilian settlement made fresh fruit and vegetables available widely. Improvements in firearms technology made them safer and more reliable to use, though still the soldier always risked his life when careless with his weapon. Even the best of weapons still required maintenance to keep them clean and in good working order, for until the last lance was laid down, a time could come very suddenly when the soldiers were going to need them.

Above: *The railroad made survival that much easier for all as it made resources more speedily and readily accessible. The Transcontinental Railroad revolutionized the settlement of the West. Here a Union Pacific train crosses the bridge at Devil's Gate in the Utah territory.*

CHAPTER EIGHT

Men at War

*"Each column will be able to take care of itself – chastising the Indians
should it have the opportunity."*
(Gen. Sheridan in a note to Gen. Sherman, less than a month
before the Battle of Little Bighorn)

*I*T TOOK WHITES some time to accustom themselves to the kind of
warfare to be expected from Indian foes. The idea of swift hit and
run raids, satisfaction with limited damage or booty, and then a
disappearance just as speedy, ran counter to Anglo ways of war. For
the Indians, however, it was an instinctive means of survival.
Without any of them knowing it, the natives were just the latest
practitioners of an evolutionarily ancient mode of warfare that
allowed for resolution of conflicts and blowing off the energy and
passion of inevitably excitable young men, without endangering the
greater survival of the species.

Native peoples everywhere in the world practiced the same kind
of warfare, just as did lesser primates. Aroused animosities led to
carefully planned raids, but carried out at minimum risk to the
attackers. And then the fighting ended as swiftly as it had begun
once there were a few kills or captures. The concept of crushing
victory, of one army all but wiping out another, or of one people
erasing another from existence, was simply foreign to the Indian
nature, though on rare occasions it had happened. The complete
annihilation of George A. Custer's command of the 7th Cavalry on
the Little Bighorn was an anomaly in Indian warfare, made possible
by overwhelming numbers, opportunity, and perhaps some little
learning of the white man's more ambitious battle aims. Despite
Hollywood portrayals, Indians wiped out very few wagon trains, but

took advantage of isolated wagons or straggling emigrants to make their kills in ones and twos.[1]

For the native warrior, individualism was just as important as cooperation. A cult of bravery dictated that he must take great risks in order to prove his manhood and elevate his standing in his tribe, and so that he could sing his own praises in the war songs he would compose thereafter. Trophies were more important than nebulous political or territorial aims in a war, whether against whites or fellow natives. Horses, women, scalps, and the like were more prized than actually taking a foe's life. In fact, the best achievement of all was not to kill an enemy, but to get close enough in battle to touch him with a "coup" stick or a lance, and then, having "counted coup" on the foeman, to escape. Indeed, given the confusion and noise, and often the darkness, leaders maintained very little control over their men in the fight. Thus, while an Indian attack began as a closely planned and coordinated affair, at the first war whoop it

Above: *For men at war in the West, reactions needed to be swift and innovations plenty. A horse could become excellent defensive cover if necessary, or it could suddenly bolt in panic and abandon its rider to an unkind fate. Knowledge of animals as well as countryside and weapons was essential to survival.*

disintegrated into as many individual battles as there were warriors.[2]

The pre-battle ritual

Part of what helped the warrior survive was that very ceremonial nature of his warfare. Once it was determined that an attack was to be made, he observed a set of elaborate preparations, some ritual and others very practical. First the war leader exhorted his braves to take action, whipping up their enthusiasm, their anger, and also their ambition for achievement. Tribal war totems such as special arrows or bison heads were brought out and displayed to invoke their "medicine." The young men dressed themselves in the special regalia of their several warrior societies, drawing strength from the deeds of earlier members, and encouraging renewed valor in a spirit of competition with other societies within the tribe. The societies had trained the young men for this moment from adolescence, teaching them the skills of the hunt, strength and accuracy with bow and

Below: *Among the most feared of the Plains tribes were the Comanche, the most fearless horsemen on the continent, shown here in a ritual dance with pipes, spears and lances, and their little war shields. For three centuries they represented one of the major challenges to white survival in the West.*

arrow, swiftness with a tomahawk. Now some of them might take sweat baths to purify their bodies and spirits, purge themselves with emetics, or fast, and often keep their distance from the impure association of women. Almost all preparations included a war dance, a powerful group enterprise performed to incessant drums and punctuated by speeches and revelations of visions by their elders.

As a result, when an Indian went off to fight, he was probably better prepared spiritually and psychologically than any other fighting man on the planet, and that gave him an edge on survival that could and did make up for disparity of numbers and weapons. En route to battle, the war party stayed low, moving when possible through gullies and ravines, avoiding ridge lines where they might be silhouetted against the sky and spotted. On the prairies, warriors on foot could cover themselves in bison hides as camouflage, and as a precaution against an enemy crossing their trail behind them and coming up on them by surprise, they attached animal tails to the heels of their moccasins so that the fur obliterated their prints on dusty ground. Finally, having come close to their foe, they were sure to wear their war paint, another ritual that had the added benefit in some instances of acting as unintentional camouflage, aided by the warriors' stripping down to bare essentials so that they did, indeed, blend into the landscape.

Weapons of the Indians

Plains Indians, once they mastered the horse, became accomplished light cavalry, but their weapons had to become smaller to be wieldy on horseback. Bows became shorter, and once-large shields were reduced to rawhide discs on wooden frames, which the warrior held in front of his chest while riding into battle. Once firearms became available, virtually all native tribes sought

Left: *One of the reasons the Spaniards first allowed American settlers to come into Texas was so that the Yankees would provide a buffer between New Spain and the Comanches of the Plains. Once these Indians obtained horses, they became a terror to all who infringed on their domain.*

Right: *The Northern Cheyenne, allied with their cousins the Sioux, were magnificent Plains warriors. Some carried clubs like this sandstone-headed war club with an ornately beaded handle.*

Far right: *More obviously functional, and even more intimidating, was the tomahawk. This iron tomahawk on wooden handle was mass-produced as trade goods by whites, not realizing that some would be used against them.*

Right: *A Sioux tomahawk, also a trade item, has been decorated with a beaded fob. The pipe bowl on the opposite side of the haft from the blade was sometimes functional, but more often decorative and to provide balance.*

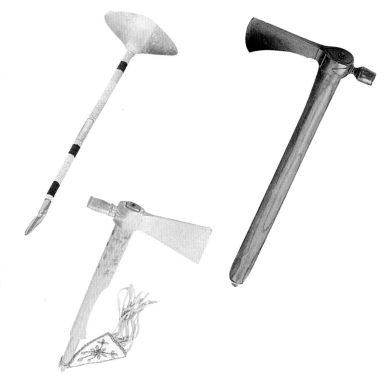

Above: *A Sioux bow covered in a mountain lion-skin sheath that both protects the wood from moisture and weakening chips, but also displays the valor of the warrior who killed the lion itself.*

them and learned their use in order to even the odds with the whites, sometimes becoming excellent marksmen. But whatever the weapon in his hand, the fighting native stayed constantly in motion, up and down in the brush, darting and dodging back and forth, to make himself as elusive a target as possible. As soon as he had his trophies or counted as many coups as seemed prudent, he melted back into the shadows and raced for home.[3]

The principal foe

When the native peoples encountered the white man west of the Mississippi, and it emerged that he was to be their principal foe, their own blood feuds diminished as more and more of them made common cause against a common threat. And thus the object of most warriors' attention in their fighting lives in the 19th century was either the white civilian or, to a lesser extent, the United States Army, each of which developed its own means of surviving the threat posed by the native peoples. The first whites, the brigades of Mountain Men and the like, adapted largely to emulate Indian modes of warfare, if not their spiritual ceremonies, but still in the end they relied on numbers, organization, and technological advantages. As the frontier became more and more settled by less experienced whites in the days of the emigrant trains and afterward, numbers and firepower became even more important. A Mountain Man might be setting traps much of the day, but every moment of his life in the wild was a preparation for surviving against whatever came at him. A farmer or stock raiser, by contrast, spent most of his time at the plow, or mending fences, planting and harvesting, and a host of other domestically necessary chores that did nothing to ready him to fight. Thus he had to depend upon meeting a native threat with greater manpower and firepower in order to compensate for vastly lesser experience and skill at warfare.

Below: One way the military coped with the danger posed by hostile natives was to remove them from their environment. Some Apaches were sent to prison in Florida, among them Geronimo. These Arapaho, Caddo, Cheyenne, Kiowa, and Comanche warriors are incarcerated at Fort Marion at Saint Augustine, and clothed in army surplus clothing.

Some of the earlier pioneers remembered the technique of corralling their wagons for protection at night, and surrounded their homes or settlements with rough stockades when danger was imminent. As communities grew, that became impractical, of course, but still even a lonely settler's soddy or abode house could be a formidable defense. One of the

Above: *When the call of danger reached the military, the command for "boots and saddles" saw troopers like these cavalrymen riding out of Fort Bowie, Arizona, on the road to the point of threat.*

most famed of all frontier combats occurred in 1874 in the "Battle of Adobe Walls," when a handful of men, including buffalo hunter William Dixon and future lawman and sports writer Bartholomew "Bat" Masterson, for several days defended themselves against hundreds of Indians behind the thick mud walls of an adobe building.[4]

Far more often, though, civilians provided for their own survival by staying vigilant and informed, and putting themselves out of harm's way in time of danger. When rumors of raiding natives circulated through the settlements, farmers removed their families to the nearest town, or better yet army post, knowing that Indian attacks on such places were almost unheard of. Survival, in short, lay mainly in not fighting, for in most instances the settler was likely to be outnumbered and cut off from support.

As their numbers grew, however, and as those of the Indians dwindled, later in the century civilians did make preemptive strikes of their own, by forming themselves into militia and putting themselves loosely under the command of an elected leader, usually a former officer in the Civil War. But these raids were not so much for defense and survival as for retaliation and intimidation on bands of natives who left reservations, or isolated individuals who stole livestock. Even then, such raids were in themselves a measure of survival if they discouraged the Indians from further depredations.

Below: *This is the typical easterner's impression of a frontier fort under attack, one that has lasted thanks to motion pictures and romantic novels. In fact, very few Army posts were ever attacked. Fewer still were palisades of upright logs as rudely constructed as the one in this romanticized 1870s painting by Charles Schreyvogel.*

Right: *Two Buffalo Soldier troopers of the 9th and 10th United States Cavalry. While they got the standard equipment of white cavalrymen, they received much inferior treatment, yet still performed a valuable service in the contest with hostile tribes who thought their curly hair resembled that of the bison, hence their nickname.*

The frontier army

But chiefly settlers relied on the frontier army for their protection, and that organization brought a radically different set of skills and traditions to the western battleground. Armies worked by rules, numbers, and efficiency. They built forts to control transportation trails, and to provide safe harbors for civilians in dangerous times. They built roads and bridges to get their firepower deep into Indian country more swiftly. They scattered their forces over more than a hundred frontier posts, most of them able to support others on little notice. Most of all, whatever they did, it was done systematically, which may certainly have left little room for flair or dash, but which also greatly reduced risks to the soldiers' survival and that of those whom they were there to protect.

Most engagements between the army and the natives were hit and run, especially if initiated by the Indians themselves. Sniping from ambush, an arrow or a bullet sent out of a thicket or from atop a

Below: Famed Western artist Frederic Remington's 1907 study "On the Southern Plains" shows a somewhat idealized view of cavalrymen charging toward a foe. Such actions were few, and usually at dawn and done by surprise. Indians preferred not to risk open massed battles.

Above: *One major exception to Indian fighting tactics was the massive attack on George A. Custer and 200 men of his 7th Cavalry on the Little Bighorn in June 1876, a testament to the danger of taking military superiority over the Indians for granted. Edward S. Paxton's painting of the scene became very popular, however inaccurate it may have been.*

butte, was a far more common hazard than a massed attack such as that which overwhelmed Custer. Better weaponry, discipline, and teamwork by squads or companies were usually enough to defend against that sort of thing. More often than not, when the soldiers were outside their garrison, it was they who were on the offensive. Using Indian guides, they too worked to achieve surprise. However, when they attacked, it was for a much more sustained engagement, expecting to inflict heavier losses, and if possible with the intent to follow up by pursuing the foe until captured or dispersed. In short, the frontier army fought less for temporal gains than for long range goals.

Soldiers, too, sought to surround a foe, or else immobilize him with his back to a river or bluff. Then the age-old tactic of rank after rank of soldiers firing ordered volleys could do its work, making up in mass of fire what it might lack in accuracy, and counting on the

Left: *One of the soundest tactics for white survival in the contest against the natives was to employ native scouts and guides, like this Apache, who mixes the uniform of his employers with his own native garb. The best way to find a foe was to use one of his own to locate him.*

Above: *Several Mescalero Apache army scouts pose in their mixture of uniform and tribal clothing, their weapons displayed proudly, and again a mix of native and Army gear. These men joined with Sergeant F. W. Klopfer, of the 4th Cavalry, shown in fringed buckskins, to work for their mutual survival in the Apache wars.*

noise and terror to demoralize the foe. The camaraderie among soldiers also encouraged able-bodied men to attempt to rescue the wounded, or to stand and fight to protect the fallen, just as Indians did. And certainly there were occasions, as at Sand Creek, Colorado, in 1864, or on the Washita River in 1868, when the army managed to stage both a surprise and a massacre, killing hundreds. In both of those instances, it was the unhappy lot of the Cheyenne chief Black Kettle to be on the receiving end.[5]

Moreover, it is significant that in the few major battles that Indians fought and won – and in the resultant "massacres" that followed as with Custer in 1876, or the massacre of Captain W. J. Fetterman and eighty troopers near Fort Phil Kearny in 1866 – they

Right: *The people the frontier military had to protect were settlers like these Minnesota families who are refugees from the 1862 Sioux uprising that saw several hundred of their neighbors killed before the Army, distracted by the Civil War, was able to put down the hostiles.*

first managed either to surround the soldiers, or else force them to dismount and take shelter behind rocks and brush, or behind their own horses, which they shot. It was sound defensive posture for the troopers, but it denied them their one means of mobility and maneuver. Their being surrounded, especially in rough terrain, made impractical the sort of massed volley firepower that was their other psychological and offensive asset.[6] That was all the lesson most troopers needed to make sure they did not squander the surest means of survival available to them – numbers, mobility, and weaponry. Not only were they the characteristics of frontier warfare that gave the whites victory, but also the ones that in the end spelled the certain doom of the native peoples.

Above: *Among the most wily and deadly foes of all natives was the Chiricahua Apache Geronimo, standing in the center in front of the mounted man. The amount of Army and white civilian clothing his warriors wear is testimony to those who have already fallen to their guns.*

Left: *United States Cavalry troopers pose beside a mountain cannon near the Pine Ridge Sioux reservation not long before the last gasp of Indian resistance exploded at Wounded Knee. Failure to be ready helped lead to the disaster there, a reminder if any were needed that on the frontier survival was always at risk.*

CHAPTER NINE

The End
of the Frontier

"The more I looked the more the panorama unfolded."
(A teenager inspired by Montana, Frederic Sackrider Remington,
creator of 2,700 paintings and drawings)

*H*OW DRAMATICALLY the requirements of survival changed as the end of the century approached, and with it the juxtaposition of several vital influences. For a start, by the 1890s the continental United States was settled and all of it either carved into states or else territories for which statehood was barely a decade away. There was no more frontier. Even though there were still substantial parts of the geography that had not been accurately mapped, still the mountains no longer posed challenges to transportation. The gaps and passes were known, the major rivers had been bridged, and the railroad had long since spanned the continent. Men and women could go where they wished, or at least get close enough in some degree of comfort that the only real travel hazard they faced was a final leg by wagon – and soon enough by automobile and even airplane.

Men knew where the dangers lay and had enough information to cope with or avoid them. At the same time, the last of the Indian conflicts ended with the quashing of the Ghost Dance movement in December 1890. There would be no more battles fought on the continent, and the native peoples, if still sullen and understandably resentful, no longer posed a threat to the collective or even the individual safety of the whites. Their hunting grounds had been broken to the plow, and the swords into plowshares.

By this time, survival had taken on an entirely different caste. The disappearance of hostile foes meant that the old requirements of stealth and surprise were no longer required except by those for whom hunting now was sport. Indeed, except in the more remote farms and among the last individualistic holdouts, of those who chose the lonely mountains for their final homes, very few needed to rely on their wits for meat. The spread of the huge livestock ranches in Texas and the new Midwest, combined with the expanding tentacles of the railroad network, meant that commercially raised beef could be brought to local markets. Advances in the technology of preservation in the meat packing houses of Chicago and Kansas City made it possible for reasonably fresh tasting meat to reach even the most remote settler's cabin.

Instead, now the white men and women of the West fit one or more of a new set of definitions. They were farmers, livestock raisers, or city dwellers, merchants and clerks and laborers. Survival now was an occupational matter, and much more a case of preserving property and quality of life, than life itself. It called for no less ingenuity. Indeed, survival for some now depended more heavily than ever on developing technology, though now it was tools and machines rather than weapons, and of course that relentless organization that characterized the military, now applied to processes of merchandizing and supply.

Above: Following the end of hostilities, for Indian shamen like Wovoka, of the Paiutes, seated here, one great challenge was to preserve old tribal ways in a new and unfamiliar world.

Above: *In the aftermath of the awful tragedy at Wounded Knee, where 125 Indians and 25 soldiers lost their lives, their deaths ended the centuries-long contest for survival between their peoples. Hereafter, each had to face new dangers and learn new skills in the never-ending contest with the land.*

The cattlemen and wheat farmers

It was the cattlemen who regarded themselves as the new lords of the wide open spaces. By 1900 the great cattle drives were over as the railroad brought the market to the herd instead. Now the cowboys did not roam over whole states, but still they had to practice their trade often on vast ranches, even though fences now proscribed their territory. Even the small cattle raiser faced many of the same hazards. They all still spent a lot of time outdoors. They had to be wary of snakes and dangerous beasts from bears to wildcats. Their own horses, if not well tended, could break down and leave them isolated. Their weapons now were branding irons, fence cutters and pliers, though still they needed that six-shooter on occasion when confronted by a dangerous animal. But for them, now, all their hazards were occupational. For them, in a way, the frontier ended even more completely than it did for the farmers.[1]

The wheat farmer out on his claim in western Kansas, or the corn grower in Nebraska, could trade his woodsman's and Indian lore for increased knowledge of the environment. The weather was still a mystery to him, but to what observations there were as to its course, he paid particular attention. Water was vital, and he had to have rain for his crop to survive. Drought was beyond his control, though increasingly farmers turned to the ground at least for subsistence moisture. Small windmills began to dot the landscape, one to every farm in time, pumping through wind power at least enough water from wells to supply people and animals. No grower could store enough water to get his crops through a prolonged drought, but he could care for at least enough to keep the family vegetable garden growing. If he had livestock and faced the risk of the watercourse on his property drying up, by now he knew enough to create earth reservoirs to capture and store rainwater. The great dust storms of the 1930s were still more than a generation in the future, but already

Below: *The Plains and prairies had new masters now, the cowboys who tended the herds of livestock and drove them to railheads for market. The environment was the same and so were many of the dangers faced, but the cattlemen developed their own particular skills both for their jobs and their own welfare.*

Right: *The cowboy riding through thickets and brush had to worry about his legs being scratched, and the result was chaps like this pair made of dog hide. The hat protected his eyes from sun and his head from heat, while the bandanna could be pulled up over his nose to keep out the trail dust on a drive.*

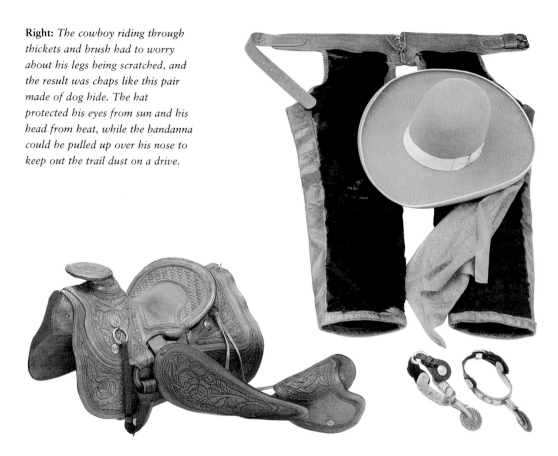

Above: *The most utilitarian and versatile tools of the cowboy were his saddle and spurs. This ornate tooled California saddle has "tapaderos" – protective leather leg guards. The saddle kept rider on horse and provided a base for his belongings in saddlebags.*

there were occasional hints of what could happen when water became too scarce.

Even when water was abundant, the settler still faced other uncertainties. Plagues of grasshoppers and other insects periodically swarmed across large portions of the plains and prairies. All he could do was stand in the fields with his family and wave blankets and sacks to try to scare them away, usually to no avail. The more progressive and affluent could buy netting to spread over the grain, keeping the insects out, and by the end of the century commercial manufacturers had begun to produce not only chemical and organic fertilizers to promote crop growth, but also the beginning of pesticides to kill those that came to plunder.

There were still hazards to the physical safety of the settlers, of course. If none now was likely to starve or die from thirst, there were still natural hazards. Tornadoes were killers, and provident settlers learned to dig "storm cellars" or caves beneath their houses for shelter, often using them for cool storage for preserved fruits and vegetables now that home canning became a common practice in

Below: *A major tool of the cowboy's trade was the branding iron, like this one that would have burnt an "M" into the thick hide of a calf. Marking animals was the only sure way to protect one's animals from straying into another's herd.*

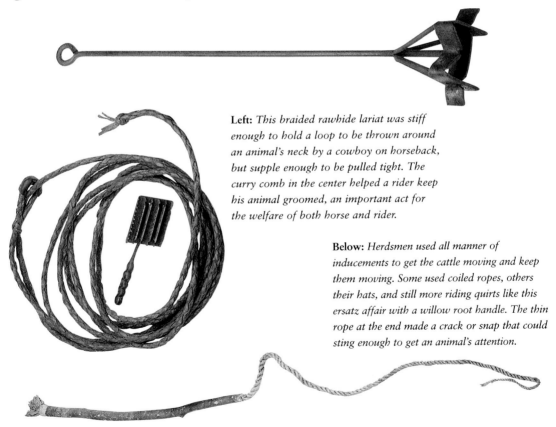

Left: *This braided rawhide lariat was stiff enough to hold a loop to be thrown around an animal's neck by a cowboy on horseback, but supple enough to be pulled tight. The curry comb in the center helped a rider keep his animal groomed, an important act for the welfare of both horse and rider.*

Below: *Herdsmen used all manner of inducements to get the cattle moving and keep them moving. Some used coiled ropes, others their hats, and still more riding quirts like this ersatz affair with a willow root handle. The thin rope at the end made a crack or snap that could sting enough to get an animal's attention.*

almost every farm house. Torrential rains could produce flash floods that were deadly if the farmer did not set his house up a bit from the ground or dig ditches to channel the water away from house and animals. The sun, too, could be as much friend as foe. Now he had domesticated animals like cows and pigs and chickens, and they needed some kind of shelter from the elements, and so barns became ubiquitous. By 1900 one more weapon of survival came into his hands, as wire stretching slowly across the country began to bring the telephone into even some farm homes, from which a call could summon a doctor or midwife to tend a birth or men and injury.

And always the farmer had to be careful, for he was still a long way – often many miles – from real relief. Carelessness with an axe or hay fork could bring death or serious injury. A fall from a roof could mean a broken back. A kick from a horse in an unguarded moment could cause concussion, broken bones, or worse, and with medical help often half a day distant or more, any injury posed a real threat. Thus every settler's house now had its little store of patent medicines, many of them useless, but a few like iodine offering at least an ally in the war against infection.

Below: Even without threats from hostile natives, still the people now faced the eternal hazards of the landscape, and especially the livestock raisers who had to care for hundreds or thousands of animals. Water was a perennial concern, as for these sheep watering on the Powder River.

Left: *The men and women breaking the soil to plant their crops and build their homes in the West had to content with animals, insects, sand storms, tornadoes, droughts, torrential rains, and every other manner of hazard. The challenges to survival for farmers have been eternal since man first domesticated crops.*

Meanwhile, for his spiritual survival, the church – in a host of denominations, mostly protestant except among Catholic ethnic groups like Hispanics, or among the more recent Asian immigrants – provided the comfort needed to battle the isolation, and to find meaning to act as a palliative when the random acts of nature and climate wrought senseless hardship.[2]

Towns and cities

The growth of towns and even cities also worked to encourage the survival and longevity of the settlers. Towns brought tradesmen and specialists, so the farmer no longer had to be the Jack-of-all-trades. The towns hosted most of the schools, and entertainments like theater, as well as, of course, the seamier sides of civilization, the drinking halls and brothels and gambling dens – and in those latter, men and women sometimes risked their survival to the hazards of civilization, drink, violence, disease, and destitution. Thus it was fortunate that most of the churches, too, were in or close to the towns and villages. But most of all, the town meant community spirit, an end – even if only temporarily – to the isolation of the homestead, and a connection to the larger culture and civilization of which the people of the disappearing frontier were so much a part.[3]

Some of those towns appeared for very special reasons linked to a local – and temporal – resource. Discovery of gold and silver in

Above: *Charles M. Russell painted his "A Disputed Trail" in 1908, and it captures one of the hazards faced by any who attempted to infringe on a bear or a mountain lion's territory.*

California and Nevada brought tens of thousands of would-be-millionaires to the foothills and mountains of the Rockies and the Sierras. Many perished from carelessness to natural hazards. Many more simply went back home penniless with dashed dreams. But for those who persevered, boom towns emerged at Silver City and Placerville and a host of other such towns, their prosperity brief, and doomed to flicker out when the ore veins disappeared.

These were communities geared to serve the exploiters, not those who came to make new communities, yet they, too, were necessary to the survival of the prospector out on his "diggings," or to service the needs of the larger commercial mining establishments. In both, men had to learn new disciplines, about how to burrow and live beneath the ground, how to avoid cave-ins, or how to spot "color" in the bottom of a pan. The immigrants, largely Chinese, who flocked to towns to find work also had to learn how to survive in hovel conditions, on tiny wages, and as well how to survive in an environment of prejudice different even from that faced by the Indians.

The end of the frontier affected no one so much as it did the native peoples, though by 1900 their whole way of life had already been turned inside out, and along the way perhaps two-thirds of their people had been killed by disease and wars. Survival for most now was

Left: For security, as well as comfort and prosperity, settlers increasingly came to rely on settlements, then communities, then towns and cities, like Liberal, Kansas, shown here just days after its founding in 1886. What began in tents soon became solid structures, schools, churches, even opera houses.

a matter of accommodation to reservation living, with much of their necessities being furnished by Washington. But this was at the cost of their ancient ability to take care of themselves, with all the consequent damage that did to self-respect and esteem. To be sure, even at this late date there were still a few holdouts who lived a wild Stone Age existence in the mountains in the Sierras, but they would die out rapidly, simply unable to survive. The last of them, a Californian Yahi Indian named Ishi, would leave the wild in 1911 and adopt white ways, effectively putting an end to the millennia-long history of the independent native peoples of North America. Enemies of the Indians now were dejection and depression, poor health, poverty, and often indifference from the agencies created to make their lives better. Survival was still a struggle, only now against new foes.[4]

As for the men whose job it had been to contain and disarm the native peoples, the soldiers of the frontier, their job, too, changed dramatically when they were no longer needed to keep

Below: Laramie, in the Wyoming Territory in 1868, revealed the face of a frontier community's rapid growth. Brewers, tobacconists, jewelers, banks and more now stood side-by-side with the stereotypical saloons. Wherever the settlers went, they brought their old civilization with them.

Above: *Part of what helped to spread white civilization so rapidly and dramatically were the tentacles of their railroads like the Central Pacific. The industry and technology that could span this valley could bring goods to almost any place in the West.*

Right: *Those who faced the toughest survival in the new West were those to whom it once belonged. Displaced, disinherited, often dispersed, people like these Kiowa, Comanche, Cheyenne, and Arapaho prisoners in Florida.*

peace. By 1900 they were mostly gone to other posts as international affairs began to transfer America's defense interests abroad. For those who remained, survival was no longer in question, except perhaps at the hands of a flooded stream or some other natural calamity as the military took on more of its earlier role of taming the landscape rather than its people.

By 1900, the American West had undergone in the 19th century perhaps more change and upheaval than that ever experienced by any other geographic mass of its size in so short a period of time. In 1800 the number of whites in the region was at best a few hundred. By 1900 it was in the millions. The population of the Indians had declined to a pitiful remnant, as had the once mighty herds of bison. The rivers were not yet tamed, but dams were on the way. Rails had scarred the backbone of the land and

Left: *Irving R. Bacon's allegorical 1906 painting "Conquest of the Prairie" shows the result of the contest for survival, as Indians stand at bay while the buffalo run past them and a wagon train brings new settlers to occupy what had been their land.*

Below: *A West being tamed, scarred by the iron rails of the railroad, its rivers spanned by bridges, its soil broken by plows.*

brought steam everywhere. Electricity was not far behind, and the sounds of hammer and nail replaced the reports of hunters' guns and soldiers' muskets.

Yet survival was still the essential preoccupation of the people of the West, regardless of race, color, or creed. But it was a new kind of survival, requiring new skills no longer predicated on conquest, defense, or even exploitation in the old sense of the term. Rather, surviving in the coming centuries meant even more rapid adaptation in the face of technological explosions, cultural redefinitions, and America's sudden leap to the front boards of the world stage.[5]

Endnotes

CHAPTER ONE
1. Editors of Time-Life Books, *The Way of the Warrior* (Alexandria, VA, Time-Life Books, 1993), pp. 129-31.
2. Francis Haines, *The Plains Indians* (New York, Thomas Y. Crowell, 1976), pp.234-39.
3. John Manchip White, *Everyday Life of the North American Indian* (New York, Holmes and Meier, 1979), passim.
4. Roland Dean Vangen, *Indian Weapons* (Palmer Lake, CO, Filter Press, 1972), passim.
5. Colin Taylor, *The Warriors of the Plains* (New York, Arco, 1975), passim.
6. Richard Irving Dodge, *Our Wild Indians* (Freeport, NY, Books For Libraries, 1970) p.245.

CHAPTER TWO
1. Paul E. Hoffman, *A New Andalucia and a Way to the Orient: The American Southeast During the Sixteenth Century* (Baton Rouge, LA, Louisiana State University Press, 1990), pp. 3-4.
2. John C. Ewers, "Symbols of Chiefly Authority in Spanish Louisiana," in John Francis McDermott, ed., *The Spanish in the Mississippi Valley* (Urbana, IL, University of Illinois Press, 1974), pp. 272-73.
3. Louis Houck, ed., *The Spanish Régime in Missouri* (Chicago, University of Chicago Press, 1909), II, pp. 170-71.
4. Lawrence Kinniard, ed., *Spain in the Mississippi Valley, 1765-1794* (Washington, Georgetown University Press, 1946-1949), I, pp. 229-30, 236.
5. Ewers, "Symbols," p. 272.
6. Marcel Giraud, *A History of French Louisiana* (Baton Rouge, Louisiana State University Press, 1974), I, p. 64ff.

CHAPTER THREE
1. Gary E. Moulton, ed., *The Journals of the Lewis & Clark Expedition, Volume 4 April 7-July 27, 1805* (Lincoln, NE, University of Nebraska Press, 1987), pp. 15, 18, 128-29, 276.
2. Ibid., pp. 139, 310, 436, 457.
3. Ibid., pp. 145, 293.
4. Ibid., 309.
5. William H. Goetzmann, *New Lands, New Men: America and the Second Great Age of Discovery* (New York, Viking, 1986), pp. 118-20.
6. Ibid., pp. 122-24.
7. Robert M. Utley, *A Life Wild and Perilous* (New York, Henry Holt, 1997), pp. 59-60, 90-99.
8. Ibid., pp. 57-58.

CHAPTER FOUR
1. Robert Utley, *A Life Wild and Perilous* (New York, Henry Holt, 1997), pp.86-87.
2. Paul Chrisler Phillips, *The Fur Trade* (Norman, OK, University of Oklahoma Press, 1961), II, pp. 536-38.
3. Alpheus H. Favor, *Old Bill Williams, Mountain Man* (Norman, OK, University of Oklahoma Press, 1937), p. 207.
4. Robert Campbell, *The Rocky Mountain Letters of Robert Campbell* (New York, published privately, 1955), pp. 7-11.
5. Washington Irving, *The Adventures of Captain Bonneville, U.S.A., in the Rocky Mountains and the Far West* (Norman, OK, University of Oklahoma Press, 1986), p. 70.
6. Robert Utley, *A Life Wild and Perilous* (New York, 1997), p. 151.
7. David J. Weber, *The Taos Trappers: The Fur Trade in the Far Southwest, 1540-1846* (Norman, OK, University of Oklahoma Press, 1968), p. 170.
8. Robert Utley, *A Life Wild and Perilous*, p. 14.

CHAPTER FIVE
1. Samuel Rutherford Dundass, *Journal of . . .* (Steubenville, OH, privately published, 1857), p. 8.
2. John D. Unruh, Jr., *The Plains Across: The Overland Emigrants and the Trans-Mississippi West, 1840-1860* (Urbana, IL, University of Illinois Press, 1979), pp. 118-20.
3. Ibid., pp. 131-32.
4. Ibid., p. 156.
5. Ibid., pp. 164-66.
6. J. Orin Oliphant, ed., "Passing of an Immigrant of 1843," Washington Historical Quarterly, XV (July 1924), pp. 206-207.
7. Unruh, *Plains Across*, p. 175.
8. Margaret Frink, *Journal of the Adventures of a Party of California Gold-Seekers* (Oakland, CA, privately published, 1897), p. 28.

CHAPTER SIX
1. William C. Davis and Joseph G. Rosa, *The West* (London, Salamander Books Ltd., 1994), pp. 75-75.
2. William C. Davis, *The American Frontier* (London, Salamander Books Ltd., 1992), pp. 55-57.
3. Richard A. Bartlett, *The New Country: A Social History of the American Frontier, 1776-1890* (New York, Oxford University Press, 1974), pp. 170-71.
4. Ibid., pp. 215-18.
5. Davis, *Frontier*, pp. 135-36.
6. Craig Miner, *West of Wichita* (Lawrence, KS, University Press of Kansas, 1986), p. 171.

CHAPTER SEVEN
1. Richard Bruce Winders, *Mr. Polk's Army: The American Military Experience in the Mexican War* (College Station, TX, Texas A&M University Press, 1997), pp. 109-110.
2. Ibid., pp. 111-12.
3. Nancy Alpert Mower and Don Russell, eds., *The Plains...by François des Montaignes* (Norman, OK, University of Oklahoma Press, 1972), p. 106.
4. Winders, *Polk's Army*, p. 127.
5. Samuel Chamberlain, *My Confession: The Recollections of a Rogue* (Lincoln, NE, University of Nebraska Press, 1987), pp. 186-87.
6. Robert Ryal Miller, *The Mexican War Journal and Letters of Ralph W. Kirkham* (College Station, TX, Texas A&M University Press, 1991), p. 9.
7. Mary Lee Spence and Donald Jackson, eds., *The Expeditions of John Charles Frémont: Volume 2, The Bear Flag Revolt and the Court-Martial* (Urbana, IL, University of Illinois Press, 1973), pp. 108, 111.

CHAPTER EIGHT
1. John D. Unruh, Jr., *The Plains Across: The Overland Emigrants and the Trans-Mississippi West, 1840-1860* (Urbana, IL, University of Illinois Press, 1979), pp. 189-91.
2. Robert Utley, *Frontiersmen in Blue* (New York, Macmillan, 1967), pp. 7-9.
3. The Editors of Time-Life Books, *The Way of the Warrior* (Alexandria, VA, Time-Life Books, 1993), pp. 78-92, 144-56.
4. William C. Davis and Joseph G. Rosa, *The West* (London, Salamander Books Ltd., 1994), p. 75.
5. Stan Hoig, *The Sand Creek Massacre* (Norman, OK, University of Oklahoma Press, 1963), p. 158ff.
6. Robert Utley, *Frontier Regulars* (New York, Macmillan, 1973), pp. 259-61.

CHAPTER NINE
1. Richard A. Bartlett, *The New Country: A Social History of the American Frontier, 1776-1890* (New York, Oxford University Press, 1974), pp. 228-34.
2. Ibid., pp. 216ff.
3. Ibid., pp. 343ff.
4. William C. Davis and Joseph G. Rosa, *The West* (London, Salamander Books Ltd., 1994), pp. 166-67.
5. William C. Davis, *The American Frontier: Pioneers, Settlers, and Cowboys 1800-1899* (London, Salamander Books Ltd., 1992), pp. 248-50.

Index

Adobe Walls, Battle of, 106
Air rifles, 37
Alaska, 31
Aleut, **14**, 31
Apache, 18, **105, 111, 112,** 113
Apache, Chiricahua, **113**
Apache, Mescalero, **112**
Arapaho, 70, **105, 124**
Arikara, 42
Arizona, **65**
Arkansas River, 39, 48
Army, U.S., 88 et seq, **88**
Artillery, **91**

Bacon, Irving R., **125**
Bear maw's cap, 7
Bear skins, 21
Bear traps, 53
Beaver pelts, 44, 47
Bent's Fort, **48**
Bering Strait, 31
Bierstadt, Albert, 56
Bison/buffalo, **12,** 23, 30, 72, 75 et
    seq, 78, **79**
Bison/buffalo dung (for fires), 85,
    85
Bison/buffalo skins, 21
Black Kettle (Cheyenne chief), 112
Bluff City, Iowa, 87
Boats, 30
Boats (Indian), 20
Bone Express, 62
Boots, soldiers', **89, 90**
Boulder, Colorado, **71**
Bowie, James, 6
Bows and arrows (Indian), 9, 17,
    17, 18, **18, 18,** 52, **104**
Branding irons, **119**
Bridger, Jim, **42,** 58
British explorers, 32
Buckskin clothing, **38**
Buffalo (see Bison)
Buffalo hunters, 74, **75,** 76, **76**
    et seq, **78,** 106
Buffalo Soldiers, 88, **108**

Caddo, **105**
California, 27, 28, 31, **31,** 33, 42,
    57, **60, 62**
California, Gold Rush, 122
California saddle, **118**
California Trail, 33, 59, **65**
Canada, 30
Canadian River, 95
Cannibalism, 71
Canoes (Indian), 20
Canoes, 30, **38,** 46
Canteen, Model 1858, **92**

Carolina, South, 24
Carson, Christopher "Kit," 42, 43,
    45
Cattle drives, 116
Cattlemen, 116 et seq
Cattlemen's equipment, 116
Cavalry, U.S., **90,** 93, 100, 106,
    108, **109,** 112, **113**
Central Pacific Railroad, 124
Charbonneau, Toussaint, 35
Cheyenne, 72, **104, 105,** 112, **124**
Cheyenne headdress, **9**
Cheyenne, Northern, **9**
Chicago, 115
Chicora, 24
Chinese prospectors, **61,** 122
Chippewa, 23
Cholera, 61
Civil War, 43, **91, 93,** 98, 107, **112**
Clark, William, 33, 34 et seq, **34,**
    65
Class system (Spanish), 27
Climate, 9, **18, 23, 41,** 104
Colorado, 7, 48, 53
Colorado River, 65
Columbia River, 33, 65
Comanche, 42, **102, 103,** 105, 124
Communications (Indian), 22
Conchiti, 24
Conestoga wagons, **62, 66**
Continental Divide, 42
Cooper, James Fennimore, 12, 22
Corn, 30, **30,** 83, 116
Corps of Discovery, 34, **34**
Cowboys' clothing and equipment,
    118
Cree, **16**
Cree snowshoes, **22**
Creek, **29**
Creoles, 27
Crooks, General George, **95**
Crow, **17,** 24, **25,** 42
Cunningham Gulch, Colorado, 7
Curry comb, **119**
Custer, George Armstrong, **93,**
    100, 110, **110,** 112

Dakota Badlands, **95**
Dakotas, 77
Darwin, Charles, 11
de Champlain, Samuel, **13**
de la Mothe Cadillac, Antoine, 13,
    14
de Quejo, Pedro, 24, 25
Deerskin clothes, **16**
Deppe, Ferdinand, 27
Devil's Gate, Utah, **99**
Dixon, William, 106

Dodge, Colonel Richard, 23
Donner party, 65, 71
Drought, 116, 117
Dugout pits (for buffalo hunting), 77

English explorers, 26
Eskimo, 31
Europeans, 24 et seq
Eyesight (Indian), 23

Farmers, 72
Ferris, Warren, 51, 55
Fetterman, Captain W. J., 112
Fish, 23
Fish traps, **21**
Fishing, **21**
Fishing in ice, **8**
Flathead, 51
Florida, 29, 105, **124**
Folk medicines, 7
Food preservation, 21
Fort Bowie, Arizona, **106**
Fort Clatsop, **33**
Fort Kiowa, 42
Fort Marcy, Santa Fe, **94**
Fort Marion, Saint Augustine, **105**
Fort Phil Kearny, 112
Fort Ross, California, 31, **31**
Forty-Niners, **60**
Frémont, John C., **43,** 97, **98**
French explorers, 26, 29 et seq, 32
Front Range, Rocky Mountains, 64
Fur traders, 31

Gatling gun, Model 1875, **93**
Geronimo, **105,** 113
Ghost Dance movement, 114
Gila River, 65
Glass, Hugh, 43
Gloves, Bearskin, 55
Gold, 57
Gold camps, **61**
Gold prospectors, 122
Gold Rush, 59, **60**
Great Plains, 39, 40, 72
Gross Ventre, 51

Haida canoes, **20**
Harpers Ferry, Virginia, 36
Hawken Rifles, 54
Hazards, Natural, 119 et seq
Henry "Yellow Boy" rifle, **52**
Hogan (tent), 17
Horses, 18, 20, 54, 59, **101, 103**
Hudson's Bay Company, 47
Humboldt River, **65**
Hunter skills, 77
Hunters, **64,** 72 et seq

Hunting, 26, **54**
Hunting skills, Native American, 15
Huron, **13**
Illinois River, 30
Independence, 33, 57, 58, **62**
Indian
    attacks on wagon trains, 68
        et seq, **69, 70**
    camp tools, **17**
    foods, 35
    guides, 110, **111**
    medicines. 35
    pre-battle rituals, 102
    remedies, 35
    shields, 103
    war tactics, 100 et seq, 109
    weapons, 102, 103 et seq, **104**
Indians, 12 et seq
Ingelik, **21**
Iroquois, 12, **13**
Ishi, (Californian Yahi Indian), 123
Iwoa, 56

Jackson Hole, Wyoming, 45
Jamestown, Virginia, settlements,
    25, 30
Jefferson, President Thomas, 34

Kansas, 33, 56, 58, 77, 80, 83, 115
Kettle Falls, Columbia River, 23
Kiowa, **105,** 124
Klopfer, Sergeant F. W., **112**
Knapsack, Model 1855, **92**
Knives, **17, 41,** 54
Koryak, **8**
Kuntz, Jacob, 37

Lances. 18, **41,** 70
Languages, 51
Laramie, Wyoming Territory, 123
Lariats, **119**
Latter Day Saint elders, 80
Leutze, Emanuel, **11**
Lewis, Meriwether, 33, 34 et seq,
    34, 65
Liberal, Kansas, **123**
Little Bighorn, 100, **110**
Livestock ranches, 115 et seq
Long, Major Stephen H., 40, 57
Louisiana, 6
Louisiana Territory, 30, 32, **33,** 34
    et seq, **34,** 40,
Louisiana Purchase, 88

Massacres, 112
Masterson, Bartholomew "Bat,"
    106
Mestizos, 27, 28

Index

Mexican revolution, 28
Mexico, 20
Minnesota, **112**
Mississippi, 7, 32, 33
Mississippi River, 6, 26, 72, 88, 105
Mississippi Valley, 29, 30
Missouri River, 33, 40, 42
Mohawk, 19
Mojave (Mohave), 41, 42
Montagnais, **13**
Montana, 77
Mormon Trail, 65
Mormons, 80
Mountain gun, Hotchkiss 2-pounder, **93**
Mountain Men, 42, 43, 44 et seq, 56, 57, 58, 72, 89, 105
Mules, 54, 59, 98
Musket, English Tower Flintlock, **19**
Muskets, 13, **34**, 57
Muskets, Flintlock, 54
Muskets, Matchlock, 25
Muskets, Smoothbore, 54

Napoleon, Emperor, **89**
Natchez, 6
Native Americans, 12 et seq
Navajo, **29**
Navigation aids, 35
Nebraska, 40, 56, 77, 116
Nevada, 65
Nevada desert, 33
Nevada gold prospectors, 122
New York, 57
Nez Perce, 51, **52**

Ohio, 57, 83
Oklahoma, 77
Old Spanish Trail, 65
Omaha, 33, 45
Ontario, 45
Oregon, 61, **62**, 64, 67
Oregon territory, 56
Oregon Trail, 33, 59, 65
Ottawa, 13, **13**, 14, 15

Pacific coast, 31, 56
Pacific Ocean, **20**
Paiute, 64, 66, 115
Pawnee, **64**
Paxton, Edward S., **110**
Peninsulares, 27
Peonage, 28
Pierre's Hole, Wyoming, 51
Pike, Lieutenant Zebulon, 39
Pike's Peak, 39
Pima, **18**

Pine Ridge Sioux reservation, **113**
Pistols and revolvers
   Aston .54 caliber, 90
   Colt Model 1860, **90**
   Colt Single Action Army, 78
Placerville, 122
Plains, 72, 84, **117**
Plains Indians, **12**, **23**, 80, **102**
Plains warriors, **104**
Plants, 26, 72, 84
Plymouth settlements, 25
Pomo, **21**
Pork eaters, 47
Powder Face (Arapaho chief), 70
Powder horns, 54
Powder River, 120
Prairie schooner (wagon), **66**
Pratte & Company, B., 51
Presidios, 28
Prospectors, 7
Pumpkin, 30, **30**

Quantsino, 36

Rabbit sticks, **14**
Racism, 61
Railroads, 57, 80, 99, 115, **124**, **125**
Red River, 39, 40
Religions, 27, **27**
Remington, Frederic Sackrider, **109**, 114
Rendezvous, 45
Rifle-musket, Model 1861, **91**
Rifles, 57, 62
   Black powder, 44
   Flintlock, 40
   Hawken, **54**
   Henry, **52**
   Kentucky, 54
   Model 1803 flintlock, 36, **37**
   Pennsylvania, 54
   Percussion, **49**
   Sharps, 74, **74**, **75**, 76, **78**
   Spencer, **78**, **93**
   Winchester 1873, **78**
Roadside telegraph, 62
Rocky Mountains, 33, 39, 44, 65
Roots and herbs (for food), 30
Rush's Pills, 36
Russell, Charles M., **38**, 122
Russian explorers, 26, 31

Sacagawea, 35, **37**
Salt Lake, 42
San Diego, 65
San Francisco, 31
San Francisco Bay, 28

Sand Creek, Colorado, 112
Sandbar Fight, 6
Santa Fe, 39
Santa Fe Trail, 33, 65
Scalping, **96**
Schreyvogel, Charles, **107**
Seminoles, 29
Serra, Juniperro, 27
Settlers, 72 et seq
Settlers' churches, 87
   communities, 86, 87
   crafts, 80 et seq
   homes, **82**, 83 et seq, 105
   livestock, 83 et seq, **86**
   medical supplies, 120
   religious worship, 121
   tools, 80, **81**
   water supplies, 85
Sharps Rifle, 74, **74**, **75**, 76, 78
Sheridan, Kansas, 76
Shields (Indian), 29
Shoes/brogans, soldiers', **89**, 90
Shoshone, 66
Shotguns, 57
Siberia, 31
Sierra Mountains, 42
Sierras, 65, 123
Silver City, 122
Sioux, 67, **95**, **104**, **112**, 113
Sioux City, 33
Skinning animals, 55
Skinning knives, 77, **78**
Slavery, 25, 28
Smith, Captain John, 30
Smith, Jedediah, 40, **41**, 57
Smith, Tom, 55
Smoke signals, 22
Snake River, 65
Snowshoes, **16**, 20, **22**, **23**
Sod houses, 83 et seq, **84**
Soddies (shelters for buffalo hunting), 77
Soldados levies, 28
Soldiers'
   health, 95 et seq
   organization, discipline, 97
   rations, 94
   uniforms and equipment, 89, 90, 91, **91**, 92, **92**
South Pass, 42, 65
Southwest, 28, **41**
Spaniards, 18, **18**, 24 et seq, **103**
Spanish explorers, 32
Spanish missions, 28
Spanish settlers, 27
Spear Society, 70
Spears, **14**, **23**
Spencer repeating rifle, 78, 93

St. Joseph, 57, 58
St. Louis, 33, 34, 57
Stalking game, 26
Steamboats, 57
Stockmen, 72
Storm cellars, 119
Sublette, William, 42, 58

Taaiyalone Mesa, 28
Taos, Mexico, 45
Texas, 6, 77, **95**, **103**, 115
Tomahawks, 17, **18**, **19**, 20, 103, **104**
Towns and cities, 115 et seq, 120 et seq
Trade goods, 35
Trading with Indians, 25, 30
Transcontinental Railroad, 99
Trappers, 44, 47, 53, 55, 57
Traps, 47, **47**, 53, 105
Travois, 50, **95**
Truckee River trail, California, 64
Twain, Mark, 12
Typhoid, 85

Union Pacific trains, 99
United States Army, 88 et seq
Utah, **80**
Utah desert, 33
Utes, 48

Voyageurs, 31, **34**, **45**, **46**

Wagon trains, 58 et seq, **62**, 100, 105, **125**
Wagons, 58, 66 et seq, **66**, 67, **69**, **71**
War club (Cheyenne), **9**
Washita River, 112
Water supplies, 117 et seq
Weapons (for hunting), **14**
Weapons (Indian), **17**
Wigwam, **171**
Williams, Will "Old Bill," 42, 45, 47
Winchester 1873 rifle, **78**
Wind River Mountains, Wyoming, 59
Wintu, **17**
Women, the role of, 82 et seq, **85**, 87
Wounded Knee, **113**, 116
Wovoka (Indian shamen), 115
Wyoming, 77

Yahi, 123
Yellowstone River, 33
Yuma warriors, **18**

Zuni, 28